MORE CHOICES
for a Healthy Low-Fat You

Cheryl D. Thomas Peters, Dietitian
James A. Peters, M.D., Dr.P.H., R.D.

REVIEW AND HERALD® PUBLISHING ASSOCIATION
HAGERSTOWN, MD 21740

Editors . . . . .Jeannette R. Johnson and Patricia Fritz
Copy Editor . . . . .Jocelyn R. Fay
Cookbook Designer . . . . .Meyer Design
Art Director . . . . .Robin Meyer
Photographer . . . . .Paul Poplis
Food Stylist . . . . .Carmen Hines
Assistant Food Stylist . . . .Kathy Walsh

The authors assume full responsibility for the accuracy of all facts and quotations as cited in this book.

R&H Cataloging Service

Peters, Cheryl Thomas, 1962-
Peters, James A., 1951-

    Choices for a low-fat you

    1. Vegetarian cookery.   I. Title.

        641.5636

ISBN 0-8280-1306-3

DEDICATION

I have dedicated each of my books to someone special in my life—to my mother, Carol Sims-Thomas, who patiently taught me the art of cooking and the joy of entertaining; to my daughter, Cherié, that she might share in my joy of food styling and preparation; to my son, Kent, because of his exceptional enjoyment of healthy foods and his ability to critique my recipes constructively.

This book is dedicated to my father, Kenneth D. Thomas, who inspired me to believe that I could achieve anything I put my heart into. He has encouraged me to write each of my cookbooks and to use my talents for God. My successes in life have been greater because of his constant motivation and inspiration. I love you, Daddy!

ACKNOWLEDGMENTS

Our gratitude to all those who contributed their talents to make this book a success . . . to our families and friends for contributing ideas and inspiring our books, and to our patients and seminar attendees, who have been our "living textbooks" and have taught us the direct benefits that can be achieved by making healthy choices.

Contents

Introduction 4

Nutrition and Lifestyle Healthy Weigh Plan 5

Breakfast. 26

Lunch 38

    Sandwiches 39

    Sensational Main Dish Salads 48

    Soups 56

Dinner. 62

    Pasta Recipes 63

    Rice and Couscous Recipes 72

    Potato Recipes 88

    Mexican and Legume Recipes 94

    Pizza Recipes 102

Dessert 110

Variations and Substitutions 120

Pantry and Smart Shopping Tips 128

Nutritional Analysis 136

Index of Recipes 142

Introduction

The emphasis of this fourth cookbook by Cheryl D. Thomas Peters focuses on achieving and maintaining a permanent healthy weight. The recipes place special attention on high-flavor, wholesome foods. All the recipes are low-fat, low-cholesterol, and, when prepared with the nondairy option, cholesterol-free. Other features include both low-fat dairy and nondairy options, menu planning tips, and nutritional analysis.

Cheryl is a dietitian with a B.S. in nutrition and dietetics from Loma Linda University. She and her husband, James A. Peters, work together in their Nutrition and Lifestyle Medical Clinic in Calimesa, California, where they work out healthy lifestyle, exercise, and nutrition treatment plans for patients desiring to lose weight or manage other chronic conditions. Dr. Peters, who wrote the Nutrition and Lifestyle Healthy Weigh Plan material in this cookbook, is board certified in preventive medicine and holds a second doctorate in public health and health promotion. The focus of their medical practice is the prevention and treatment of chronic medical conditions.

Weight management has been a special interest, as it is at the heart of preventive medicine. According to the most recent guidelines of the National Institutes of Health (1995) and the American Health Foundation, 59 percent of Americans are overweight. Excess weight contributes to a number of chronic diseases and is thought to be a major contributing factor in the premature deaths of more than 300,000 people each year. The solutions are not difficult, but they require persistent and consistent application of healthy lifestyle behaviors.

Misinformation often misleads and confuses people who are trying to lose weight. Presented on the following pages is a simple, straightforward, medically sound plan that has helped many people lose weight. The proper diet is one that should be permanent and that promotes optimal function and health, not simply weight loss.

Losing weight in a healthy way involves eating a healthy, low-fat, high-complex-carbohydrate diet. It involves exercising on a regular basis and developing the right mental attitude.

These factors are the same ones that help lower cholesterol and blood pressure, that lower the risk for heart disease, and that help to reverse or prevent adult-onset diabetes.

Weight is fundamentally a study of the body's energy management system. Weight management involves finding the right balance of energy intake and energy expenditure. Doing this correctly will result in better health.

At the same time, it should be fun. And by all means, the health-promoting diet should taste good! The recipes in this book have been tested in the kitchen and at the table by both liberal and finicky eaters. We hope you will find it a satisfying and tasty experience as you make better choices for a low-fat you.

NUTRITION AND LIFESTYLE HEALTHY WEIGH PLAN

Welcome to the **Nutrition and Lifestyle Healthy Weigh Plan**. The treatment of weight-related problems should always be done in a manner that is consistent with improving one's overall health and well-being. Our goal is to help you lose weight in a steady, safe fashion with results that last for life.

WEIGHT LOSS FOR LIFE!

The healthy way to achieve one's best body weight requires doing healthful things. This includes proper nutrition, exercise, and psychological factors. Those who have weight-related medical problems should work with their physician and dietitian.

Appropriate exercise and nutritious, well-balanced meals are the cornerstone to good health and safe weight loss. If you are on prescription medications, periodic monitoring by your doctor is necessary, because some adjustments in medications may be needed as you lose weight.

YOUR WEIGHT AND YOUR HEALTH

Excess body fat has been shown to be a significant risk factor for a number of chronic diseases. Too much body fat increases the risk of developing adult-onset diabetes (also known as noninsulin dependent diabetes mellitus–NIDDM), heart disease, high blood pressure, and joint-related problems, as well as psychological and social problems. While weight alone is not the only cause of these chronic diseases, it is an important contributing factor.

Most chronic diseases have several factors that contribute to the onset of the disease. The more factors a person has, the greater the risk of developing a given disease. Fortunately, if one modifies or lessens any one of these contributing factors, the risk is correspondingly reduced. Achieving and maintaining one's ideal weight is a most important health activity. In fact, decreasing one's weight by 20 to 30 pounds can reduce hypertension, improve blood sugar control, decrease the risk of diabetes, and/or decrease the risk of complications from diabetes.

HOW MUCH SHOULD I WEIGH?

How much one should weigh is affected by several factors: gender, height, frame size, age, and genetic factors. Women weigh less than men for any given height, because they have less lean body mass. The taller one is, the more he or she can weigh and still be in good health. Likewise, the larger the frame size, the more weight that is allowed. Weight and height tables usually take these factors into account in determining the appropriate weight for any given height. Occasionally one's best weight may be a little above or below the indicated values because of genetic and other factors that are not accounted for.

The most commonly used weight and height table is from the Metropolitan Life Insurance Company. The weight for a given height that is associated with the best longevity is considered to be one's best, or ideal, body weight. But keep in mind that these tables are most representative of those who apply, and are accepted, for life insurance and may not represent those who never apply, or are never accepted, for insurance.

As one gets older, weight frequently increases, largely because of the effects of aging and subsequent slowing of the metabolic rate. Very likely the increased weight with age corresponds to an increasingly sedentary lifestyle, with no corresponding adjustments in the way one eats.

FIND YOUR BODY MASS INDEX [BMI]

HEIGHT

WEIGHT

Table 1

WEIGHT	5 FT						HEIGHT IN INCHES						6 FT							
	56	57	58	59	60	61	62	63	64	65	66	67	68	69	70	71	72	73	74	75	76
100	22	22	21	20	20	19	18	18	17	17	16	16	15	15	14	14	14	13	13	13	12
105	24	23	22	21	21	20	19	19	18	18	17	16	16	16	15	15	14	14	14	13	13
110	25	24	23	22	22	21	20	20	19	18	18	17	17	16	16	15	15	15	14	14	13
115	26	25	24	23	23	22	21	20	20	19	19	18	18	17	17	16	16	15	15	14	14
120	27	26	25	24	23	23	22	21	21	20	19	19	18	18	17	17	16	16	15	15	15
125	28	27	26	25	24	24	23	22	22	21	20	20	19	18	18	17	17	17	16	16	15
130	29	28	27	26	25	25	24	23	22	22	21	20	20	19	19	18	18	17	17	16	16
135	30	29	28	27	26	26	25	24	23	23	22	21	21	20	19	19	18	18	17	17	16
140	31	30	29	28	27	27	26	25	24	23	23	22	21	21	20	20	19	19	18	18	17
145	33	31	30	29	28	27	27	26	25	24	23	23	22	21	21	20	20	19	19	18	18
150	34	33	31	30	29	28	27	27	26	25	24	24	23	22	22	21	20	20	19	19	18
155	35	34	32	31	30	29	28	28	27	26	25	24	24	23	22	22	21	20	20	19	19
160	36	35	34	32	31	30	29	28	28	27	26	25	24	24	23	22	22	21	21	20	20
165	37	36	35	33	32	31	30	29	28	28	27	26	25	24	24	23	22	22	21	21	20
170	38	37	36	34	33	32	31	30	29	28	27	27	26	25	24	24	23	22	22	21	21
175	39	38	37	35	34	33	32	31	30	29	28	27	27	26	25	24	24	23	23	22	21
180	40	39	38	36	35	34	33	32	31	30	29	28	27	27	26	25	24	24	23	23	22
185	42	40	39	37	36	35	34	33	32	31	30	29	28	27	27	26	25	24	24	23	23
190	43	41	40	38	37	36	35	34	33	32	31	30	29	28	27	27	26	25	24	24	23
195	44	42	41	39	38	37	36	35	34	33	32	31	30	29	28	27	27	26	25	24	24
200	45	43	42	40	39	38	37	36	34	33	32	31	30	30	29	28	27	26	26	25	24
205	46	44	43	41	40	39	38	36	35	34	33	32	31	30	29	29	28	27	26	26	25
210	47	46	44	43	41	40	38	37	36	35	34	33	32	31	30	29	29	28	27	26	26
215	48	47	45	44	42	41	39	38	37	36	35	34	33	32	31	30	29	28	28	27	26
220	49	48	46	45	43	42	40	39	38	37	36	35	34	33	32	31	30	29	28	28	27
225	51	49	47	46	44	43	41	40	39	38	36	35	34	33	32	31	31	30	29	28	27
230	52	50	48	47	45	44	42	41	40	38	37	36	35	34	33	32	31	30	30	29	28
235	53	51	49	48	46	44	43	42	40	39	38	37	36	35	34	33	32	31	30	29	29
240	54	52	50	49	47	45	44	43	41	40	39	38	37	36	35	34	33	32	31	30	29
245	55	53	51	50	48	46	45	43	42	41	40	38	37	36	35	34	33	32	32	31	30
250	56	54	52	51	49	47	46	44	43	42	40	39	38	37	36	35	34	33	32	31	30
255	57	55	53	52	50	48	47	45	44	43	41	40	39	38	37	36	35	34	33	32	31
260	58	56	54	53	51	49	48	46	45	43	42	41	40	38	37	36	35	34	33	33	32
265	60	57	56	54	52	50	49	47	46	44	43	42	40	39	38	37	36	35	34	33	32
270	61	59	57	55	53	51	49	48	46	45	44	42	41	40	39	38	37	36	35	34	33
275	62	60	58	56	54	52	50	49	47	46	44	43	42	41	40	38	37	36	35	34	34
280	63	61	59	57	55	53	51	50	48	47	45	44	43	41	40	39	38	37	36	35	34

DETERMINING YOUR BMI

BMI = weight (kg)/height (meters)²

This chart determines your BMI so that you can use the chart on page 7. Find your height in inches across the top of Table 1 (above) and then locate your weight down the left-side column. Where the weight and height boxes come together, that is your BMI.

There is a strong genetic disposition for weight-related problems. Those whose parents are overweight often have a greater tendency to be overweight themselves. Such persons may have to work much harder to maintain a normal weight than others, because of the genetic tendency predisposing them to weigh more. Others, despite a lot of hard work and decreasing calorie intake, may find it impossible to reach their textbook "normal" weight and must settle for a slightly more generous standard. This more generous standard may actually be their normal, and getting lower than this may not be in their best interest.

It isn't always fair. However, proper eating and regular physical activity can greatly offset hereditary tendencies for obesity. Regardless of the weight loss achieved, a better level of health can be experienced simply through the process of making healthier choices of eating better and exercising more.

DETERMINING YOUR BODY MASS INDEX [BMI]

One of the best ways to determine one's optimal weight is by determining at which weight the least risk for developing weight-related diseases occurs. The goal is to maintain the weight that poses the least risk to one's health, yet "feels" right. The body mass index (BMI) is one method for evaluating the proper weight for a given height. BMI is an index number (a ratio of weight/height) that has been used in nutrition research to determine which height/weight relationships are safer, and which numbers correspond to greater risk of illness.

The BMI is calculated by dividing one's weight (in kilograms, kg) by one's height (measured in meters and squared): **BMI = weight (kg)/height (meters)^2**. To make it easier, refer to *Table 1* on page 6.

WHAT THE BMI MEANS TO YOU

A number of large research studies have correlated BMI with the risk of developing weight-related diseases, such as diabetes, hypertension, and heart disease. In the chart below, the BMI (on the horizontal) is plotted versus the mortality ratio (on the vertical). The mortality ratio indicates the risk or chance of dying from a weight-related illness for any given BMI, with a ratio of 1.0 being the standard risk of dying if one were at the normal weight.

BMI RISK

Locate your BMI on the bottom horizontal line. Follow that line up to the graph line. This is your risk for developing a weight-related illness. The darker the red area, the greater your risk. If your BMI is above 30, you can greatly improve your health with even a modest weight loss.

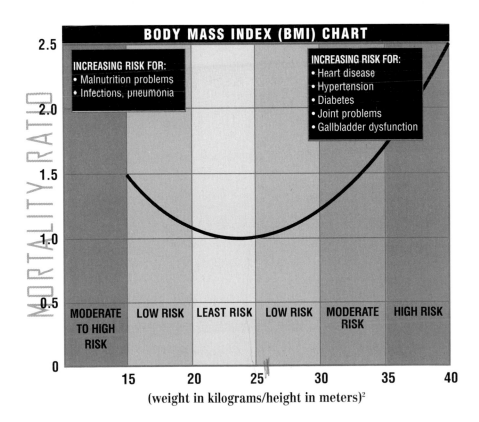

Healthy Weigh Plan

The Body Mass Index (BMI) Chart *(page 7)* shows that as the BMI increases, risk of dying also increases. It also shows that the safest weight range corresponds to a BMI of 20 to 25. The risk increases above 25, slowly at first, then more dramatically as the BMI goes above 30. Conversely, as one's weight and BMI decrease, there is a corresponding decrease in risk.

It is helpful to remember that for those with BMI values above 30, the greatest decrease in risk occurs with the initial weight loss. Maintaining a 20- to 30-pound loss can result in significant long-term health benefits.

The only way to lower one's BMI or weight is to burn more calories than one takes in. The intake of calories occurs only through diet. So eating fewer calories becomes an important consideration.

The other important consideration is using or burning calories. Burning calories occurs in two ways:

1. calories are consumed in the process of keeping our body alive; and
2. calories are used in the process of powering our muscles, thereby allowing us to move about.

Three fourths or more of the calories burned each day are simply consumed in the first process of keeping alive: heart beating, lungs breathing, liver and brain functioning, and other body functions. To burn additional calories requires effort—physical exertion. Exercise is the only way to burn more calories voluntarily.

The challenge, then, is how to eat fewer calories, yet feel satisfied and get sufficient nutrition to sustain healthy body functioning. And how to burn enough calories to help with the process and yet not spend all day exercising or suffering exercise-related injuries in the process.

First, let's look at diet.

WHAT SHOULD I EAT?

Proper nutrition involves eating enough calories and obtaining sufficient nutrients to sustain a healthy-weight body and allow us to pursue our desired activities. Therefore, the concern in nutrition is to get enough energy (calories). Our goal with weight loss is to take in fewer calories each day than we are using up. This results in a deficit and forces our body to consider using more of its energy stores (primarily fat stores).

Although our goal is to take in fewer calories, we still should take in enough every day for proper body functioning. Too few calories puts the body into starvation mode, and after about 10 days the body becomes very efficient at "living off" very few calories. The rate of weight loss begins to slow down—or even stops. If we then try to make up for this by limiting our food intake even more, the body will not only use the fat reserves for energy but also will use muscle tissue to create the necessary blood sugar to power the brain, resulting in unhealthy weight loss. At this point if we increase our food intake a little, our weight seems eager to increase again.

Occasionally there may be merit in short-term calorie restriction. This is called fasting. Fasting should not exceed one day (with no restrictions on water) and should occur no more frequently than once per week. Fasting might be useful for some as a means of maintaining a given weight; however, those with medical conditions, such as diabetes, should check with their physician first, since fasting could result in unsafe blood sugar levels.

The best weight loss plan, however, is one that lowers the energy intake level several hundred calories (or more) below that which is required for the day (after considering one's resting calorie need and daily activity level). This plan results in a more gradual weight loss with less discomfort and less metabolic stress to the body and is thought to be more permanent, since it is done more gradually and allows time for changes in lifestyle. To determine what energy or calorie needs are required to either lose or maintain weight, see *Table 2* on the following page, **"Determining Your Calorie Needs."**

153 × 9 = 1377

Table 2

DETERMINING YOUR CALORIE NEEDS

Faster Weight Loss	**Slower Weight Loss**	**Maintenance of Weight**
9 calories/lb	11 calories/lb	14 calories/lb

Multiply your current weight by 9 or 11 calories-per-pound body weight. That will give you an estimated number of total calories to consume per day that will result in weight loss.

To lose body fat requires that we encourage the body to use more of its stored fat energy. Eating fewer calories per day than the body actually needs or burning off more calories (exercising) results in some of the needed energy coming from the breakdown of fat. *(See Table 3 below.)*

You can choose which way you wish to experience your caloric deficit: eat less, or exercise more. The fact of the matter is that one should do both, since exercise is always necessary, not only for healthy and permanent weight loss, but for good health.

It is difficult, however, to achieve rapid weight loss with exercise alone, since it takes not only effort, but time. For example, to burn 100 calories by exercise requires walking 15 to 20 minutes.

Whereas, avoiding an extra slice of bread, or only 10 crackers, can result in 100 fewer calories instantly. For some, finding that extra "something" they have been splurging on each day—a soda or a chocolate bar—can make the calorie difference between weight loss or weight gain. Just one can of soda contains about 150 calories. One can per day can result in 15 pounds gained over the course of a year. Switching to a noncalorie drink, such as water, can be an easy change that provides long-term benefits.

To lose one pound a week by exercise alone requires 500 calories being expended per day, the equivalent of walking about five miles a day, five days a week. This may be fine for some, but others may not have time for this much

exercise. A combination of exercise with fewer calories eaten per day is the best choice.

The foods that are best suited for losing weight are those that contain the least amount of fat. Fat has more than double the calories per given weight than carbohydrate (starchy foods) or protein foods.

So the quickest way to reduce *calories* in the diet is to decrease the amount of *fat* in the diet. This decreases the calories but still leaves a lot of good food to eat. Typically, eating less fat results in faster weight loss.

CALORIE MATH BOX

To determine how many deficit calories per day are required to lose one pound of fat per week:

3,500 calories in a pound of fat
- 3,500 ÷ 7days = 500 calories deficit per day required
- This equals four pounds per month.

Table 3

CALORIE TABLE

Fat	.9 calories/gram
Carbohydrate	.4 calories/gram
Protein	.4 calories/gram
Alcohol (not a food) . . .	.7 calories/gram

Table 4

Remember, the fat you eat is the fat you wear.

The first rule is to avoid the visible fats in the diet: butter, margarine, cheese, and the fats in meats and dairy products. From these foods, choose those that contain the lowest fat or eat smaller servings, and eat them less often. Note that one does not have to eliminate all fat from the diet, as this results in such a strict regimen that eating is not as pleasurable, and good health is not always served.

About 20 percent of one's caloric intake should come from fat. *Table 5* will help you calculate the amount of fat grams allowed in the healthful diet.

We recommend avoiding alcohol—it not only contains a large number of calories, but it does not contribute to one's nutrient intake and can cause a multitude of health problems.

OK, so we know what to eat *less* of; what should we eat *more* of?

FOODS I CAN EAT

Fruits, vegetables, whole grains, and beans are the foods that should be eaten generously. These foods are high in complex carbohydrates (the main fuel of the body), high in nutrients, high in fiber, but low in calories from fat. One can eat these foods and feel full, yet be assured of good nutrition and still lose weight or maintain a normal weight.

More than 200 medical research studies discovered that people who eat more fruits and vegetables experience fewer heart problems and fewer cancers.

Table 5

FAT GRAM CALCULATION

- *If you are aiming for a total calorie intake of 1,500 calories, and 20 percent of these calories are from fat, then:*
  1,500 x .20 = 300 calories per day from fat

- *Since there are nine calories per gram of fat:*
  300 ÷ 9 = 33 grams of fat per day

Plant foods have *no* cholesterol and are excellent for lowering both cholesterol and weight.

You ask, But aren't starchy foods (such as bread) fattening?

Actually, no! Any excess calorie intake will be stored in the form of fat in the body, whether it comes from protein, carbohydrate, or fat. Consider what happens if we eat 100 calories more than we need for the day *(see figure below).*

If the excess calories are from fat, then 98 of the 100 calories eaten will be stored as fat, since it is already in the form of fat.

If the excess calories are carbohydrate, they must first be converted to fat.

This takes 25 percent of the calorie energy to do this; therefore, of the 100 excess starch calories eaten, only 75 calories will go to fat storage.

From this example it can be seen that carbohydrate foods are the least fattening of the foods we can eat. Furthermore, complex carbohydrates are high in fiber, water, and many nutrients. This is what helps us feel full and less hungry, yet contributes fewer calories to our diet.

The recommendations endorsed by the United States Department of Health and Human Services (HHS) and the United States Department of Agriculture (USDA) are summarized on page 13, *Table 7,* the **Vegetarian Food Pyramid**.

FAT STORAGE

100 EXCESS FAT CALORIES

98% of Calories Stored as FAT

·········· 2%

25%

If you eat 100 excess carbohydrate calories, 25% of them are used to convert carbohydrates to fat—making carbohydrates the least fattening foods you can eat.

75% of Calories Stored as FAT

100 EXCESS CARBOHYDRATE CALORIES

In making the food selections from the different groups above, strive to make the healthiest choices from each of the food groups. For example, from the grain group choose the unrefined grains, foods that are 100 percent whole wheat, or oats rather than white or enriched flour foods.

In the protein group, make more selections from beans, the soy products (such as tofu), and some of the nuts (such as almonds). Although nuts are higher in fat, they contain more of the good-quality fats that the body needs.

In the fruit and vegetable groups, favor the whole, least-processed foods. Choose a whole apple instead of apple-sauce or apple juice. The more processed, the less fiber and usually the more sugar or other additives.

From the dairy group, favor the nonfat selections. For those who cannot digest dairy products properly, or who prefer not to use them, make more selections from the dark, leafy green vegetables and fortified soy milk products. This will assure more calcium in the diet.

Following these guidelines will help you to meet the general U.S. Nutrition Recommendations *(Table 6)*. The basic nutrition message of the Vegetarian Food Pyramid *(page 13)* is that most of one's food selections should come from the foods at the base of the pyramid, represented by the largest area (bread, cereal, rice, and pasta). Eat generously from the vegetables and fruits; eat moderately from the low-fat or nonfat dairy and protein groups; and eat sparingly from the foods at the top of the pyramid—the free oils, fats, sugar, and salt.

HOW MUCH SHOULD I EAT?

1,200 calories:

The lowest amount recommended to maintain nutritional adequacy. This calorie level is appropriate for weight loss.

1,200 CALORIE DIET: 59% CARBOHYDRATE, 21% PROTEIN, 14% FAT (27 GRAMS)	Daily Total	Breakfast	Lunch	Dinner
Bread/Starch	6	2	2	2
Fruit	3	2	1	
Vegetable	3		1	2
Milk (nonfat)	2	1		1
Protein (lean)	3		2	1
Fat	2	1		1

1,500 calories:

Usually recommended for weight loss with most men. It is also appropriate for weight maintenance for sedentary women and some older adults.

1,500 CALORIE DIET: 60% CARBOHYDRATE, 22% PROTEIN, 16% FAT (35 GRAMS)	Daily Total	Breakfast	Lunch	Dinner
Bread/Starch	9	3	3	3
Fruit	3	2	1	
Vegetable	3		1	2
Milk (nonfat)	2	1		1
Protein (lean)	3	1	1	1
Fat	3	1	1	1

Healthy Weigh Plan

1,800 calories:

Recommended for weight loss for some men, especially active men. It is also recommended for more active women for weight maintenance.

1,800 CALORIE DIET: 58% CARBOHYDRATE, 20% PROTEIN, 23.6% FAT (48 GRAMS)				
	Daily Total	Breakfast	Lunch	Dinner
Bread/Starch	11	3	4	4
Fruit	4	2	1	1
Vegetable	3		1	2
Milk (nonfat)	2	1		1
Protein (lean)	5	1	2	2
Fat	4	1	2	1

2,200 calories:

Recommended for most children, teenage girls, active women, and sedentary men. Women who are pregnant or nursing may need more calories.

2,500 calories:

Recommended for teenage boys, active men, and some very active women.

Table 6

U.S. NUTRITION RECOMMENDATIONS

- Eat a variety of fruits and vegetables
- Calories to maintain normal weight
- Complex carbohydrate 50-60%
- Protein 10-12%
- Fat (total 30% or less)
  Saturated fat < 10% of fat
- Cholesterol intake < 300 mg/day
- Fiber 20-30 g/day
- Salt < 5g/day

HOW BIG IS A SERVING SIZE?

Figuring the amount of food you should eat is easier with these images as a guide:

HOW BIG IS A SERVING SIZE?	
1 ounce meat	matchbox
3 ounces meat	bar of soap
8 ounces meat	thin paperback book
medium apple or orange	tennis ball
medium potato	computer mouse
1 cup lettuce	four leaves
slice of bread	cassette tape
average bagel	hockey puck
1 ounce cheese	four dice
1 cup fruit	baseball

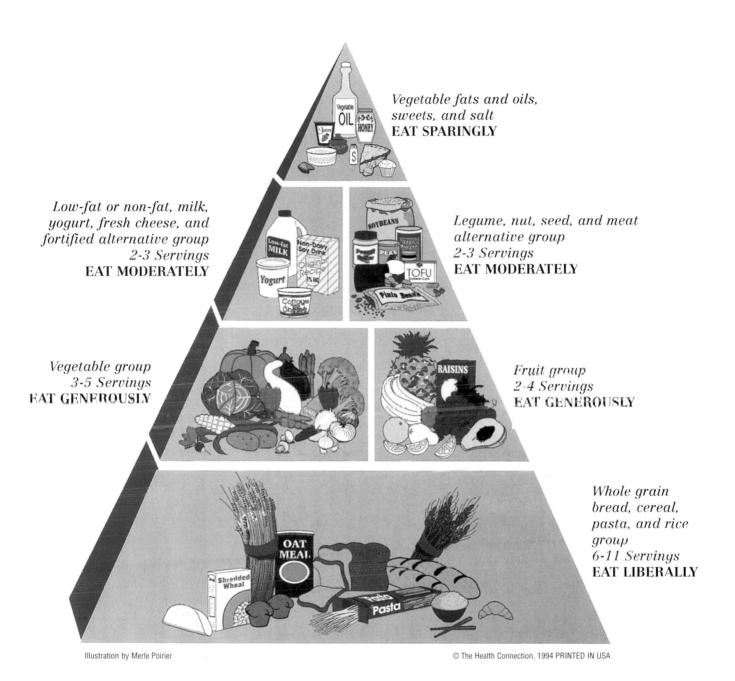

Vegetable fats and oils, sweets, and salt
EAT SPARINGLY

Low-fat or non-fat, milk, yogurt, fresh cheese, and fortified alternative group
2-3 Servings
EAT MODERATELY

Legume, nut, seed, and meat alternative group
2-3 Servings
EAT MODERATELY

Vegetable group
3-5 Servings
EAT GENEROUSLY

Fruit group
2-4 Servings
EAT GENEROUSLY

Whole grain bread, cereal, pasta, and rice group
6-11 Servings
EAT LIBERALLY

Illustration by Merle Poirier

© The Health Connection, 1994 PRINTED IN USA

VEGETARIAN FOOD PYRAMID
Table 7

Creating a Low-Fat Diet

WHAT'S IN A SERVING?

Here are some serving size examples for each food group. If you eat larger portions, count them as more than one serving. To get a balanced diet, we should eat a minimum of the lowest number of servings from the five food groups each day.

BREAD, CEREAL, RICE, AND PASTA GROUP:
(Eat 6-11 servings daily)

- 1 slice bread
- 1 ounce ready-to-eat cereal

(check labels: 1 ounce = $^1/_4$ cup to 2 cups, depending on cereal)

- $^1/_2$ cup cooked cereal, rice, or pasta
- $^1/_2$ hamburger roll, bagel, or English muffin
- 3 or 4 plain crackers (small)

BREAD, CEREAL, RICE, AND PASTA GROUP

It's hard to go wrong choosing whole-grain and cereal foods as a big part of a healthy eating style. Health experts encourage us to consider grains as the base of a nutritious diet. Not only are oats, wheat, corn, and other grains cholesterol-free, but they also contain very little fat. However, some recipes for grain foods can call for the addition of fatty ingredients. When butter, margarine, shortening, oil, or cheese are main ingredients in bread products, then breads can be quite high in fat. Some examples of items on the high-fat list include croissants, Danish pastries, doughnuts, sweet rolls, and cheese breads. For everyday eating, it's best to highlight lower-fat breads, cereals, and whole grains.

Favor Lower-Fat, High-Fiber Grain Items:

- whole-grain sandwich breads, such as wheat, rye
- whole-grain English muffins
- whole-grain hot dog and hamburger buns
- whole-grain bagels
- whole-grain pita or pocket bread
- unfried tortillas (corn, flour)
- plain pasta, noodles, rice
- oatmeal, grits, cornmeal
- dry cereals, except regular granola
- crackers (saltines, graham, melba toast, bread sticks)
- pretzels, air-popped popcorn
- fig and low-fat fruit bars, gingersnaps, vanilla wafers, animal crackers

Minimize Use of Higher-Fat Grain:

This is where we find much of the hidden fat in our diets:

- butter rolls
- cheese bread, croissants
- doughnuts
- oversized muffins
- biscuits
- convenience pasta mixes with cheese or cream sauces
- fried rice
- regular granola
- corn chips, potato chips
- butter-flavored and cheese-flavored crackers
- chocolate chip and bakery cookies, frosted cookies
- bagel chips
- french fries
- scalloped potatoes
- potato salad

FAT CONTENT OF BREAD, CEREAL, RICE, AND PASTA		
Item	Serving Size	Grams of Fat
rice, pasta, cooked	$^1/_2$ cup	trace
bread	1 slice	1
hamburger roll, bagel	1	2
English muffin	1	2
tortilla	8-inch diameter	3
crackers, plain	small, 3-4	3
pancakes	4-inch diameter, 2	3
cookies, plain	medium, 2	4
doughnut	medium	11
croissant	large	12
Danish	medium	13
cake, frosted	medium, $^1/_{16}$	13
pie, fruit	8-inch diameter, $^1/_6$	19
potatoes, scalloped	$^1/_2$ cup	4

Food Guide Pyramid, *U.S. Department of Agriculture, Human Nutrition Information Service; April 1992. Home and Garden Bulletin 249—Adapted.*

VEGETABLE GROUP:
(Eat 3-5 servings daily)

- 1 cup raw, leafy vegetables
- ½ cup other vegetables, cooked or chopped raw
- ¾ cup vegetable juice

VEGETABLE GROUP

Vegetables are naturally low in fat and contain no cholesterol. The only way to make vegetables high in fat or cholesterol is by adding toppings to the vegetables, such as butter, margarine, rich cream sauces, or large quantities of cheese added for additional flavor.

Many frozen or convenience vegetable products can be the highest in fat, because many of them come already cooked with extra fats or sauces.

Favor Lower-Fat Vegetables:

- fresh vegetables
- frozen vegetables without sauce or butter
- canned vegetables without sauce or butter

Minimize the Use of Higher-Fat Vegetables:

- frozen vegetables with cheese, cream, or butter sauce
- asparagus with hollandaise sauce
- fried zucchini, eggplant Parmesan

FRUIT GROUP:
(Eat 2-4 servings daily)

- 1 medium apple, banana, orange, nectarine, or peach
- ½ cup chopped, cooked, or canned fruit
- ¾ cup fruit juice

FRUIT GROUP

Fruits are also low in fat and cholesterol-free. The only two exceptions: coconut and avocado. Any kind of fresh or frozen fruit or juice fits easily into a low-fat diet. Whole fresh fruits (apples with skin, pears, plums, etc.) have more fiber than frozen juices or canned fruits. Soluble fiber, which is high in fresh fruits, has been found to be helpful in lowering blood cholesterol levels.

Eat a Generous Amount of Fruit:

- fresh fruits
- dried fruits, such as raisins and prunes
- canned fruits, packed in their own juice
- frozen fruits

FAT CONTENT OF VARIOUS VEGETABLES		
Item	Serving Size	Grams of Fat
vegetables, cooked	½ cup	trace
vegetables, leafy, raw	1 cup	trace
vegetables, nonleafy, raw	½ cup	trace

MILK, YOGURT, AND CHEESE GROUP: (Eat 2-3 servings daily)

- 1 cup milk or yogurt
- 1½ ounces natural cheese
- 2 ounces processed cheese

MILK, YOGURT, AND CHEESE GROUP (Calcium Group)

The milk or dairy group can be thought of as a calcium group. There are many sources of calcium other than dairy products for those who do not use dairy products or for those who have a lactose intolerance. Examples of other calcium sources: broccoli, almonds, tofu, dark leafy green vegetables, tofu or soy milk, etc.

The milk group contains foods that can be high in fat and cholesterol, so you need to be more careful when selecting foods from this group. Whole milk, for instance, carries about 8 grams of fat per cup. To decrease high fat totals, gradually wean yourself away from whole-milk dairy foods to products made with skim or low-fat milk. Start using skim milk in recipes for puddings, sauces, soups, and baked products.

Soy milk or tofu milk is also available in low-fat form. These milk substitutes are equivalent to a milk exchange if they have equal amounts of calcium as dairy milk.

Lower-fat cheeses are another way to trim the fat in the diet. Many hard cheeses carry 10 or more grams of fat in a 1-ounce portion. Use cheese minimally and avoid it altogether by using the nondairy cheese substitutes available in the Variations section of the cookbook.

Favor Lower-Fat Dairy Products:

- skim milk
- 1 percent milk
- low-fat tofu or soy or rice milk
- evaporated skim milk
- nonfat milk powder
- 1 percent low-fat or fat-free cottage cheese
- nonfat and low-fat yogurt
- reduced-fat or fat-free sour cream
- nonfat cream cheese
- nonfat or low-fat cheese
- nondairy tofu sour cream (made with low-fat tofu)
- nondairy cheese substitutes (recipes in the Variations section of cookbook)

Minimize the Use of Higher-Fat Dairy Products:

- whole milk
- evaporated milk
- sweetened condensed milk
- buttermilk made with whole milk
- creamed cottage cheese (4 percent fat)
- cream cheese
- hard cheeses, such as cheddar and Swiss
- ice cream (particularly premium)
- sour cream
- whipped cream
- half-and-half

FAT CONTENT OF MILK, YOGURT, AND CHEESE

Item	Serving Size	Grams of Fat
skim milk	1 cup	trace
1% milk	1 cup	2.6
2% milk	1 cup	5
2% milk, chocolate	1 cup	5
whole milk	1 cup	8
nonfat yogurt, plain	8 ounces	trace
low-fat yogurt, fruit	8 ounces	3
low-fat yogurt, plain	8 ounces	4
cottage cheese, 4% fat	½ cup	5
mozzarella cheese, part skim, grated	½ cup	7
ricotta cheese, part skim	½ cup	10
cheddar cheese, natural	1½ ounces	14
processed cheese	2 ounces	18
frozen yogurt	½ cup	2
ice milk	½ cup	3
ice cream	½ cup	7
premium ice cream	½ cup	14
Rice Dream 1% fat nondairy beverage	1 cup	2
tofu white milk	1 cup	5
Better Than Milk	1 cup	5
WestSoy 1% Fat Lite	1 cup	2
WestSoy original	1 cup	5
tofu whipped cream	1 tablespoon	2
tofu sour cream	1 tablespoon	3
nondairy cheese	2 tablespoons	1
(recipe in Variations section of the cookbook)		

PROTEIN GROUP
(Eat 2-3 servings daily — 5-7 Ounces Total)

Vegetarians substitute dry beans, eggs, and nuts for meat, poultry, and fish. Be sure to select lean foods from this group.

- 2 to 3 ounces cooked lean meat, poultry, or fish

(1 ounce of meat = 1/2 cup cooked dry beans, 1 egg, or 2 tablespoons of peanut butter)

PROTEIN GROUP:
MEAT OR MEAT ALTERNATIVE
(Meat, Poultry, Fish, Dry Beans, Eggs, and Nuts)

The protein group is one of the most important places to start trimming the fat in your diet. Many people are trying to reduce their intake of red meat, poultry, and fish, and choose more plant-based foods. Plant-based meat alternatives are the easiest way to cut back on fat and cholesterol in the diet. Dry beans and peas are high in protein, but much lower in fat than meat. Combined with rice or other grains, legumes, such as kidney beans or black-eyed peas, make high-quality meat replacements.

If you choose to eat meat, poultry, and fish, here are some ways to trim the fat:

- Choose select or leaner cuts of red meat such as beef round and sirloin tips
- Trim the fat with poultry by selecting younger birds, which are lower in fat
- Remove the poultry skin; white meat tends to be lower in fat
- Choose fish that is lean versus fatty. Lean fish swim closer to the bottom of the water. Examples: flounder, halibut, ocean perch, which average approximately 5 percent fat. Fatty fish live in the middle or surface of the water and are approximately 20 percent fat. Examples: salmon, mackerel, herring, tuna, sardines.

Favor Leaner Protein or Meat Replacements:

- dry beans, split peas, lentils
- egg whites
- 1 percent fat Mori-Nu tofu
- tuna, canned in water
- chicken, turkey (remove skin)
- extra-lean ground sirloin
- veal
- haddock, flounder, ocean perch

Avoid Higher-Fat Protein Items:

- prime beef, heavily marbled meats
- corned beef, pastrami
- spareribs, rib-eye roast, steak
- regular ground meat
- hot dogs, sausage, bologna
- bacon
- refried beans cooked with lard

FAT CONTENT OF PROTEIN GROUP (MEAT AND MEAT ALTERNATIVES)		
Item	Serving Size	Grams of Fat
dry beans, peas, cooked	1/2 cup	trace
egg	1*	5
peanut butter	2 tablespoons	15
lean meat, poultry, fish, cooked	3 ounces	6
chicken, with skin, fried	3 ounces	13
ground beef, lean, cooked	3 ounces	16
bologna	1 ounce	16
nuts: almonds, cashews, mixed	6 nuts	5
*Count 1 egg, 1/2 cup dry beans or peas, or 2 tablespoons peanut butter as 1 ounce of		

FATS, OILS, AND SWEETS GROUP (USE SPARINGLY)

Be careful to eat from this group very sparingly. These foods are mostly all fat. Remember: fat is 9 calories per gram of fat versus 4 calories per gram for protein or carbohydrate.

FAT CONTENT OF FATS, OILS, AND SWEETS		
Item	Serving Size	Grams of Fat
mayonnaise	1 tablespoon	11
low-fat mayonnaise	1 tablespoon	5.1
sour cream	1 tablespoon	2.5
lite sour cream	1 tablespoon	0.7
tofu sour cream	1 tablespoon	3
salad dressing	1 tablespoon	1.5
low-fat salad dressing	1 tablespoon	0.3
butter, margarine	1 teaspoon	4
cream cheese	1 ounce	10
lite cream cheese	1 ounce	4.7
frozen yogurt	½ cup	4.3
fruit sorbet	½ cup	2
chocolate bar	1 ounce	9

SALT

It is important to consume salt in moderation. Salt is an important flavor enhancer and food preserver. Because of its food-preservation qualities, salt is the leading additive in many processed foods. It often is also added at the dining table. There is enough sodium naturally present in the foods we eat and in our water supply to more than meet our daily needs.

Commonly used words for sodium to watch for on food labels:
- salt
- sodium
- brine
- broth
- cured
- pickled
- smoked
- soy sauce
- teriyaki sauce
- sodium bicarbonate (baking soda)
- sodium aluminum sulfate (baking powder)
- disodium phosphate
- sodium benzoate

To lower your salt intake, choose high-salt foods less often:
- salted chips
- salted crackers and nuts
- condiments
- cured and processed meats
- canned foods (vegetables, beans, fish)
- cheeses
- boxed convenience foods (macaroni and cheese, pasta mixes, or rice side dishes)

SALT CONTENT IN FOODS		
Item	Serving Size	Mg. of Sodium
air-popped popcorn	3 cups	0
regular microwave popcorn	3 cups	190
plain brown or white rice seasoned with herbs	1 cup	9
boxed convenience rice	1 cup	1,560
low-sodium chicken vegetable soup	1 cup	90
chicken vegetable soup	1 cup	1,068
green beans, fresh	½ cup	2
green beans, frozen	½ cup	3
green beans, canned	½ cup	170
low-sodium canned tuna	½ cup	79
canned tuna	½ cup	310
dill pickle	1 medium	418
ham	3 ounces	1,100

Creating a Low-Fat Diet

FAT-LOWERING STEPS

STEP 1

Build your meal on the grain or bread group. Double up on grains, vegetables, and fruits at mealtime. Fill up two thirds of your plate with these foods to help shift the focus away from higher-fat animal foods.

Choose whole-grain breads, cereals, and pastas, as well as legumes, potatoes, and corn. All are low in fat but high in vitamins, minerals, and fiber.

STEP 2

Practice the less-is-more approach to meat. It is best to replace meat with plant-based meat alternatives, such as legumes, dried beans, and nuts. But if you must have meat, consider using it as a garnish rather than the main course.

STEP 3

Wean yourself away from whole milk and high-fat dairy products. You get just as much calcium from skim and 1 percent milk products, with much less fat. Try the tofu or soy milk replacements for milk that provide equal amounts of calcium and protein.

STEP 4

Cook with less fat. Steam, microwave, stir-fry, roast, or grill foods. Add citrus juices and herbs for flavor instead of fat. Use vegetable cooking spray to replace margarine or oil. Use water in a nonstick skillet with a cover to steam vegetables instead of sautéing vegetables. When using added fat in cooking, canola or olive oils are preferable, because they are monounsaturated fats, which lower the low-density cholesterol.

Creating a Low-Fat Diet

STEP 5

Read labels for snacks and precooked convenience foods you buy. And follow the 3-gram rule: If a product food label has 3 grams of fat or less per 100-calorie serving, it falls within recommended guidelines for a low-fat food.

If you want snacks, make them low-fat and healthful by following the tips below:

- Keep sliced fruit, as well as whole fresh fruit, available.
- Keep prepared raw vegetables available for munching.
- Keep a variety of low-fat breads and muffins on hand.
- Snack on low-sugar cereals, either dry or with nonfat milk.
- Snack on plain low-fat yogurt or tofu yogurt (recipe in Variations section of the cookbook) with fruit, cereal, or bread.
- Freeze fruit juice to use as snacks on hot days.

STEP 6

Practice the art of fat balancing. If you do have a meal high in fat, be sure the next two are low in fat to keep your day in balance.

Meticulously tracking your food and fat calories at every meal is unrealistic. But you can learn enough food values for typical meals to help you estimate how you're doing. Remember, one sure way to curb the fat in any meal is to consume most of it as low-fat grains, vegetables, or fruits.

STEP 7

Cook onions, mushrooms, and green peppers in a pan coated with nonstick vegetable spray, not oil. Two tablespoons of oil used to sauté vegetables will carry an extra 240 fat calories; vegetable sprays add less than 10 calories of fat.

In addition to the above recommendations, we suggest the following:

- ➤ Decrease the total fat intake to 20 percent or less of the total calories.
- ➤ Increase the complex carbohydrates by 10 percent.
- ➤ Strive for as little saturated fat and cholesterol in the diet as possible.

CHOOSE MORE OFTEN	CHOOSE LESS OFTEN
baked tortilla chips	corn chips
pretzels	potato chips
bagel with fat-free cream cheese or fruit	doughnuts
baked apple or spiced applesauce	apple pie
nonfat frozen yogurt or tofu ice cream	ice cream
low-fat string cheese	cheddar cheese
soft pretzel	croissant
fruit smoothie or nonfat yogurt shake	milk shake
salsa	sour cream-based dip
frozen juice bar	ice cream bar
angel food cake	pound cake

Creating a Low-Fat Diet

FOOD DIARY WORKSHEET: DAILY FOOD INTAKE
(Photocopy for use)

BREAKFAST INTAKE

Bread/Starch Group	
Fruit Group	
Vegetable Group	
Dairy Group	
Protein Group (Meat/Meat Alternative)	
Fat Group	

LUNCH INTAKE

Bread/Starch Group	
Fruit Group	
Vegetable Group	
Dairy Group	
Protein Group (Meat/Meat Alternative)	
Fat Group	

DINNER INTAKE

Bread/Starch Group	
Fruit Group	
Vegetable Group	
Dairy Group	
Protein Group (Meat/Meat Alternative)	
Fat Group	

SNACKS, WATER, EXERCISE

| Snacks: (Time of Day) | |
| Water Intake | |

Exercise
Type of exercise and number of minutes

Building Blocks of Nutrition

CARBOHYDRATES

The carbohydrate foods are those that are found primarily in the lower half of the Vegetarian Food Pyramid. Carbohydrate foods (grains, vegetables, and fruits) are the foods to eat for the healthiest weight loss. Beans and legumes also fall into both this category and the protein category.

The carbohydrates that should be favored are the complex carbohydrates: starchy foods and unrefined plant foods that contain the fiber and all of the nutrients. Eat generously of these foods.

The simple carbohydrates are sugars. These should be limited, since they have calories, but few nutrients. Typically, simple carbohydrates are found mostly in the refined or processed foods. Table sugar and other sweets fall into this category. Unfortunately, these foods contribute as much as 20 to 30 percent of the caloric intake in most Americans' diet. Increased consumption of these foods increases dental caries, can raise triglycerides (free fat in the blood), elevates blood sugar more quickly, and challenges the insulin-producing system. (Insulin is the hormone needed to help sugar get into the cells of the body. It should be noted that when insulin levels are elevated, less fat is broken down for use as energy. This slows down weight loss and loss of body fat. One should favor more complex carbohydrates, since their effect on insulin is more moderate than with simple sugars.) A limited amount of sugar in the diet is all right, but it is best to eat it along with other foods at mealtime. This tends to slow the absorption and allow for more gradual uptake.

Complex carbohydrate foods, as found in grains and vegetables, increase the brain chemical serotonin more than high-protein or fat foods. Serotonin is a nerve chemical that signals the appetite center in the hypothalamus of the brain. When serotonin levels increase, you feel less hungry, or more satisfied with the food you have eaten.

Eat more of the fruits, vegetables, and grains, since these are the foods that naturally increase the brain's own production of serotonin, which decreases your sense of hunger.

PROTEIN

Protein is a crucial component of our diets. It is used by the body to build tissue, make antibodies to fight infection, build blood-clotting factors, and create a multitude of enzymes. Despite all of this, you do not need large amounts of protein. Notice that the protein is positioned toward the top of the Vegetarian Food Pyramid—foods that are to be eaten in moderation.

Excess proteins should be avoided, as they increase metabolic stress in the body. The nitrogen in the amino acids that make up the proteins must be eliminated from the body, putting a heavier workload on both the liver and the kidneys. This also increases the need for water, calcium, and various B vitamins. Excess protein is stored as fat, not as muscle or protein. Some popular diets urge large protein and small carbohydrate intake. This is not a healthy way to eat or to lose weight.

Proteins are made up of an arrangement of some 20 individual amino acids. Just as the 26 letters of the alphabet can make up millions of words and sentences, so the 20 amino acids form arrangements that create millions of different proteins that the body needs. The quality of a protein (how good it is) is defined by how many of the nine "essential" amino acids are present (out of the 20). The more of the nine essential amino acids present in a single protein, the higher the quality of that protein.

Because animal-based foods came from living creatures, their proteins contain high amounts of all the amino acids and therefore are considered to be high-quality proteins. However, the main problem with meat is that since it is high in protein, it is too easy to get too much. Meat is also high in cholesterol and saturated fat, fiber-free, and essentially carbohydrate-free. Concern for food safety is another issue in animal-derived foods.

Table 8

PROTEIN CALCULATIONS

Fun Protein Calculations for the Brave of Heart

- 1,200 calorie diet x 12% = 144 calories from protein foods
- Protein has four calories per gram
- 144 calories ÷ 4 = 36 grams of protein from protein foods

For these reasons, when meat proteins are chosen, moderate consumption of low-fat, properly cooked white meats (poultry without the skin) and fish would be the prudent way to eat, paying attention to recommended serving sizes.

Plant proteins offer an important protein alternative to animal-based foods. A diet favoring nuts, beans, and legumes produces protein qualities that can rival those of some meats. Combining grains with beans results in all the essential amino acids needed for health. The advantage of favoring the plant proteins is that they are high in fiber, low in fat, cholesterol-free, have reasonable amounts of complex carbohydrates, and even are proving to help lower cholesterol. Some of the soybean proteins are being found to lower the risk for some cancers, as well as to decrease menopause symptoms in women.

The bottom line: eat a variety of protein foods in moderation, and aim to get 10 to 12 percent of your total calorie intake from protein foods.

FATS

The dietary goal is to lower the total fat in the diet. This is desirable even if one is not interested in weight loss. However, fat should not be considered a "poison." It is needed by the body and plays an important role in body function. We simply do not need more than 30 percent of our calorie intake to be from fat, as occurs in the standard American diet. While eating less than 30 percent fat is healthier, we personally favor around 20 percent. For some people with severe medical conditions, short-term therapy at 10 to 15 percent of fat may be therapeutic.

There are three types of fat:

➤ saturated fat

➤ polyunsaturated fat

➤ monounsaturated fat

All of the above fats have the same number of calories per gram; however, their effects on health are different.

Saturated fats are solid at room temperature. The saturated fats are primarily found in foods from animal origin and are found to raise cholesterol levels. Long-term consumption is associated with certain cancers. It is noted that the vegetable-based fats that have higher levels of saturated fat are coconut and palm oils. However, some research has shown that saturated fat in the diet appears to raise cholesterol only if

cholesterol is also in the diet. So these two vegetable fats are less problematic if the diet does not contain other cholesterol foods, as palm and coconut oils do not contain any cholesterol themselves.

The polyunsaturated and monounsaturated fats are naturally liquid at room temperature and come primarily from plant foods. These unsaturated fats both lower cholesterol levels, but the polyunsaturated fats can lower the good (HDL) cholesterol along with the bad cholesterol (LDL). The monounsaturated fats lower only the bad cholesterol. Additionally, the monos also appear to help regulate blood sugar levels and favorably affect blood pressure.

Of the fats that we do eat, we recommend favoring the foods that contain larger amounts of monounsaturated fat. Some of the foods that have the highest amounts of monounsaturated fats are nuts, olives, and avocados. Medical research reports that resulted from the study of nuts show lowered cholesterol and fewer heart attacks in those people who include nuts in their diets.

Overall, limit the total amount of fat in the diet. But of the fats one uses, favor the nuts, avocados, olives, olive oil, and canola oil.

Benefits of Exercise

WHAT ABOUT EXERCISE?

Exercise is extremely important, not only for weight management, but for being healthy. If you are at your ideal body weight, exercise is still necessary for good health. The good news, however, is that you do not have to be an athlete to get the benefits of exercise.

The Surgeon General's Report on Exercise (1996) recommends that one's exercise be sufficient to burn 150 calories per day. This translates into approximately 25 to 30 minutes of exercise, the equivalent of walking one and one half miles per day.

An exercise program should start out gradually. Slowly increase the duration or intensity of exercise over several weeks. Physiological changes in the joints and muscles take time to occur. Exercise that is too intense or more vigorous than one is ready for can result in tissue injury and pain.

Your exercise session should include the following:

Warm-up

Warm-up exercises for five minutes before engaging in heavier or more vigorous exercise. A warm-up exercise typically consists of the same activity that you will be doing for the main exercise session (walking, biking, etc.), but at a lower intensity. This allows the joints to warm up and increase their lubrication, helping to prevent injury.

Heart rate

Exercise at your target heart rate for a sustained period of time—usually 20 to 40 minutes. The target heart rate is found by subtracting your age from 220, and multiplying by the percentage of desired exercise intensity (65 to 80 percent):

220 minus age times percent of desired exercise intensity.

If you have been sedentary for a while, then start your exercise at the 60 to 65 percent level for a week or two. Then progress to the 70 percent range for a couple of weeks before working your way up to 75 or 80 percent. Going higher than 80 percent will certainly help you become more fit, but it will not necessarily make you any healthier than working out in the 70 percent range.

The easiest rule of thumb to follow is to exercise at an intensity at which you can still talk easily to someone during the exercise session. If you feel too winded or short of breath, you are exercising too hard and should slow down.

Cooldown

This is a short period of exercise that is like the warm-up, only now it will help you cool down. During this period of time you should do some light stretching exercises of the muscles that have been used during the main exercise session. This increases flexibility and helps prevent soreness.

Frequency

You should try to get exercise every day. Benefits can be seen with a minimum of three days per week, but it is best to get four or five days of exercise per week.

A walking intensity exercise program is sufficient for most people who are working on losing weight and improving their health. If you have any medical problems, it is best to get clearance from your physician before engaging in any vigorous exercise routines. If you experience any shortness of breath or chest pain while exercising, postpone your exercising until you can consult your

ENERGY (CALORIES) BURNED PER MINUTE OF EXERCISE BY WEIGHT								
	100 lbs.	130 lbs.	150 lbs.	180 lbs.	200 lbs.	230 lbs.	250 lbs.	(Your Wt.)
Calisthenics	3.4	4.4	5.1	6.0	6.9	7.7	8.6	
Walking (level)								
2 mph	2.4	3.1	3.6	4.2	4.9	5.4	6.1	
3 mph	3.6	4.4	5.0	6.2	6.9	7.7	8.4	
4 mph	4.6	5.7	6.6	8.1	8.9	10.1	11.7	
Running (level 9 min/mi)	9.1	11.4	13.1	16.0	17.8	20.0	21.8	
Cycling								
5.5 mph (leisure)	3.0	3.8	4.4	5.3	5.9	6.7	7.9	
9.4 mph (leisure)	4.8	5.9	6.8	8.3	9.2	10.4	12.2	
Swim (sidestroke)	5.7	7.2	8.3	10.1	11.2	12.8	14.6	
Jump Rope (70/min)	7.6	9.6	11.0	13.4	14.9	16.9	18.4	
Basketball Practice	6.5	8.1	9.4	11.5	12.7	14.3	15.5	
Dancing (aerobic easy)	4.3	5.9	6.7	8.1	9.1	10.5	11.7	

Table 9

physician. Should a person decide to remain sedentary, he or she should consult a doctor also as this is probably more risky than walking.

The table above offers estimates of the number of calories expended in different kinds of activities.

BENEFITS OF EXERCISE

- Natural stimulant
- Helps elevate mood
- Helps burn more calories
- Helps decrease body fat
- Helps preserve and build up muscle tissue
- Decreases the risk of developing diabetes
- Decreases the risk of diabetes complications
- Helps regulate blood sugar levels
- Helps to lower blood pressure
- Improves function
- Lowers the risk of cardiovascular disease
- Can increase longevity by two years

Table 10

Exercise is a natural stimulant. Activity increases the metabolic rate and burns more calories. During an exercise bout and immediately afterward there is a decrease in the appetite. Exercise also facilitates the transfer of sugar into cells, so less insulin is needed. This is an additional reason why exercise helps with weight loss.

Your success is determined by the four factors diagrammed below in *Table 11*.

You cannot control genetics, but the other three sections of the circle are things that you *can* control or modify. Many find that adding a spiritual component makes a big difference in the achievement of one's health goals. For some with special conditions, the use of physician-prescribed medications may be of assistance in the initial weight-loss process, but medications should be used only after careful consideration of the

risks and benefits and in conjunction with a good nutrition and exercise plan.

The more you do correctly in the three modifiable areas—diet, motivation, and exercise—the better your results will be and the more permanent your new weight will be. For some the genetic tendency for being overweight is strong and may occupy a larger portion of the circle below. For these people more effort must be devoted toward eating right, thinking right, and exercising. For others the genetics may not be that dominating, and they may find it much easier to lose or maintain weight.

Life is not always fair. The focus of any weight program should be on the process of becoming healthier, not simply looking at the weight measured by the scale. Measure your success by checking to see if you have been making the healthiest choices you can.

➤ Have you chosen the healthiest low-fat foods to eat today?
➤ Have you avoided sweets and free sugars?
➤ Have you exercised today?
➤ Have you drunk generously of water?
➤ Have you chosen to eat more slowly, and to eat less, with more of your food being eaten earlier in the day?

If you have, then for today you are as thin (as healthy) as you can get. Focus on making the right choices, and feel successful when you make them. The weight will take care of itself when the

process of healthy choices occurs on a regular and consistent basis.

PRINCIPLES FOR ACHIEVING YOUR DESIRED WEIGHT

The more consistently you adhere to the principles listed below, the better will be your success.

➤ Eat most of your calories earlier, rather than later, in the day.
➤ Avoid eating late at night or just before going to bed.
➤ Favor more whole plant foods.
➤ Choose low-fat prepared or processed foods.
➤ Do not snack.
➤ Eat slowly and enjoy your food.
➤ Avoid the visible fats.
➤ Drink plenty of water.
➤ Exercise regularly at sufficient intensity and duration.
➤ Avoid alcohol: It is high in calories, interacts with many medications, and has many adverse health effects.

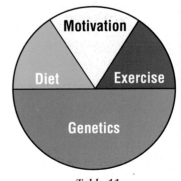

Table 11

Breakfast

Breakfast Burritos
Belgian Waffles
Apricot Sauce
Cholesterol-free Pancakes
Apple Pancakes
Low-Fat Granola
Cheryl's Almond Granola
Breakfast Shakes:
Pineapple-Banana
Peach-Berry-Banana Fruit
Breakfast Scones With Fruit
Butter and Fruit Platter:
Almond-Oat Scones
Currant-Sesame Scones
Red Berry Spread
Peach or Apricot Butter
Five-Grain Cooked Cereal
Quick-cooking Seven-Grain Cereal
Fresh Fruit Sauce
Muesli-Nut Fruit Salad

BREAKFAST BURRITOS

1 ½	pounds thin-skinned potatoes
6	flour tortillas (10 inches wide)
1	red pepper, chopped (optional)
½	teaspoon garlic powder
2	cups firm tofu *or* 16 egg whites
1	teaspoon McKay's Chicken-Style Seasoning
1 ½	cup Thick and Chunky Salsa *(p. 125)* *or* purchased salsa
½	cup Tofu Sour Cream *(p. 122)* *or* low-fat sour cream
⅓	cup green onion, sliced thin

1. Peel potatoes, halve lengthwise, and cut crosswise into ⅓-inch-thick slices. Place in 2- to 3-quart pan with water to cover and bring to a boil over high heat. Reduce heat and simmer, covered, until tender when pierced. Drain.

2. Seal tortillas in foil and warm in a 350°F oven until hot, about 10 minutes.

3. Place cooked potatoes and chopped red peppers in a nonstick skillet, sprayed with nonstick cooking spray, and cook until lightly browned, about 10 minutes. Season with garlic powder and salt, if desired. Keep warm.

4. Chop tofu and sauté in nonstick skillet sprayed with nonstick cooking spray Add ½ teaspoon garlic powder and 1 teaspoon McKay's Chicken-Style Seasoning, or to desired taste. Keep warm. (If using egg whites, beat them in a small bowl. Stir over medium heat in nonstick skillet until set. Add just the garlic powder and salt, if desired, to taste.)

5. Assembly: Lay tortillas flat. Toward one edge of each, fill equally with potatoes and tofu or egg mixture, and top with 2 tablespoons of the reserved warm chili sauce. Fold over sides and roll up tightly to enclose. Place each on a rimmed, ovenproof plate, and ladle warm Thick and Chunky Salsa on top. If the burrito needs to be warmed, place in oven at 350°F for 2 to 3 minutes until warm.

6. For a special garnishing touch, try putting the Tofu Sour Cream or low-fat sour cream in a small unpleated, heavy-duty plastic bag. Seal, then snip off a small corner of bag. Squeeze squiggles of sour cream over hot burritos. Sprinkle with green onions. Serve immediately.

Makes 6 burritos
Prep. time: 20 minutes
Cooking time: 10 minutes

MENU PLANNING TIPS

This delicious Mexican Breakfast Burrito tastes great stuffed full of vegetables and the tofu or egg white filling. Try this unique low-fat breakfast for a change at your next Sunday morning brunch. For quicker last-minute preparation, you can use a purchased salsa that you warm.

BELGIAN WAFFLES

10	ounces tofu, firm
1-2	cups tofu *or* soy *or* low-fat milk
2	tablespoons canola oil
2	tablespoons honey *or* sugar
1	teaspoon lemon juice
1	teaspoon pure vanilla extract
¾	cup whole-wheat flour, sifted
¾	cup all-purpose flour, sifted
1	teaspoon baking powder
½	teaspoon baking soda
¾	teaspoon salt
2	cups Apricot Sauce (recipe following)
1	banana, sliced
½	cup pecans

1. Preheat waffle iron.
2. Place tofu or 1 cup milk, oil, honey or sugar, lemon juice, and vanilla extract in blender and blend until smooth.
3. Sift flour, baking powder, baking soda, and salt.
4. Fold liquid ingredients into the sifted dry ingredients and mix. Add chopped nuts to batter, if desired, or use to garnish. (If using firm tofu [which has less moisture], the waffle batter could be too thick. Thin with additional milk until slightly thicker than pancake batter.)
5. Place amount of batter in waffle iron according to waffle iron directions. (Use any waffle iron for this recipe; however, a Belgian waffle iron, which takes about 4 minutes per waffle, makes a crisper waffle.) Cook until golden brown.
6. Top waffle or pancakes with the apricot sauce and place sliced bananas and nuts on top of sauce. Serve immediately.

APRICOT SAUCE

2	16-ounce cans pitted apricots, packed in fruit juice, undrained
¼	teaspoon pure vanilla extract (optional)

1. Place apricots and vanilla extract in blender or food processor and blend to desired consistency. Blend until smooth or chunky, depending upon personal preference.
2. Place on waffle according to above recipe.

Serves 6
Prep. time: 5 minutes
Cooking time:
4 minutes per waffle

MENU PLANNING TIPS

These waffles can be served with any fruit topping and a nondairy whipped topping or Tofu Whipped Cream *(p. 122)*. The fruit topping provides a sweet taste with a lot less sugar and fewer calories than traditional maple syrup. It also provides one or two fruit exchanges to help in meeting the day's requirement for fruit. Strawberries are a great replacement for the apricot sauce. Also try topping the waffles with the Red Berry Spread *(p. 34)* or the Peach or Apricot Butter *(p. 35)*.

Serves 6
Prep. time: 5 minutes

MENU PLANNING TIPS

This sauce tastes great served over waffles, pancakes, French toast, and regular toast. You could also use peaches instead of apricots. Or blend 1 cup fresh fruit until smooth and add to 1 cup chopped fresh fruit.

CHOLESTEROL-FREE PANCAKES

Serves: 6
Prep. time: 5 minutes
Cooking time: 10 minutes

MENU PLANNING TIPS

Serve with fresh or canned fruit and nondairy whipped cream or Tofu Whipped Cream *(p. 122)*. Add nuts or dried fruit for a variety in taste. Or try topping with the Red Berry Spread *(p. 34)* or the Peach or Apricot Butter *(p. 35)*.

10	ounces tofu, firm
1	cup tofu *or* soy *or* low-fat milk
2	tablespoons canola oil
2	tablespoons honey *or* sugar
1	teaspoon lemon juice
1	teaspoon pure vanilla extract
¾	cup whole-wheat flour, sifted
¾	cup all-purpose flour, sifted
1	teaspoon baking powder
½	teaspoon baking soda
¾	teaspoon salt

1. Place all the wet ingredients in blender and blend until smooth.
2. Sift together all the dry ingredients.
3. Add the sifted dry ingredients to the blender mixture and mix until smooth.
4. Preheat nonstick skillet at medium heat.
5. Pour pancake batter into skillet to make the size pancakes desired. When the top of pancake begins to bubble, turn pancake over and cook until lightly browned.

APPLE PANCAKES

Makes 14 pancakes
Prep. time: 10 minutes
Cooking time: 10 minutes

MENU PLANNING TIPS

Serve with fresh fruit or fruit sauce of choice. Peanut butter and applesauce are a nice topping for these pancakes, or the apricot sauce with the waffle recipe.

1	cup whole-wheat flour
1	cup all-purpose flour
1	teaspoon baking soda
1	teaspoon baking powder
1	teaspoon ground cinnamon
½	teaspoon salt
2	cups tofu *or* soy *or* nonfat milk
2	teaspoons lemon juice
1	teaspoon pure vanilla extract
1	tablespoon honey
1	tablespoon molasses
1	tablespoon canola oil
½	cup soft tofu, blended smooth, *or* 4 egg whites
2	cups Granny Smith apples, finely chopped

1. Combine first six ingredients in large mixing bowl; stir well.
2. Combine milk of choice, lemon juice, vanilla, honey, molasses, oil, and tofu or egg whites in small bowl; stir well.
3. Add liquid mixture to flour mixture, stirring until smooth. Fold in apple. Let stand 5 minutes.
4. Spoon about ¼ cup batter for each pancake onto a hot, nonstick griddle or nonstick skillet coated with cooking spray. Turn pancakes when tops are covered with bubbles and edges look cooked. Cook until lightly brown.

LOW-FAT GRANOLA

4	cups rolled oats
¹/₂ -³/₄	cup walnuts, coarsely chopped
¹/₄	cup unsweetened coconut, shredded (optional)
¹/₄	cup sunflower *and/or* sesame seeds
¹/₄	cup brown sugar (optional, can increase honey by ¹/₄ cup to substitute for brown sugar)
¹/₄	teaspoon salt (optional)
2	teaspoons ground cinnamon
³/₄ - 1	cup apple juice concentrate, thawed
1	tablespoon vegetable oil (optional)
4	tablespoons honey
2	tablespoons pure vanilla extract
¹/₂	cup dried blueberries *or* dried cranberries
¹/₃	cup dates *or* raisins
¹/₃	cup thinly sliced dried apricots

1. Preheat oven to 300°F. In a large mixing bowl, stir together oats, nuts, coconut, seeds, brown sugar, salt, and cinnamon.

2. In a small bowl, mix apple juice concentrate, oil, honey, and vanilla extract. Use a whisk and whip honey into the juice mixture until totally dissolved. (Note: Use 1 cup of apple juice concentrate if you prefer a clumpier granola. If you like it more like individual pieces of oats, use ³/₄ cup juice.)

3. Drizzle juice mixture over the cereal and stir to coat evenly.

4. Spread the mixture onto a large baking sheet with sides. For even baking, be sure the granola is not more than 1 inch thick. Bake for 30 to 45 minutes, stirring every 5 to 7 minutes. Add the dried fruit and bake an additional 5 minutes. The granola should be crisp and golden. Do not overcook after adding the fruit to prevent the fruit from hardening. Sometimes I soak the dried fruit in hot water for 1 minute and then drain off the water just before adding to granola to keep the dried fruit moist and better blend the flavors with the granola. Let cool. Store granola in a sealed container in the refrigerator or freezer.

5. Serve the granola with tofu, soy, or nonfat milk and top with additional fresh fruit, if desired. Makes 5 cups.

Serves 10
Prep. time: 5 minutes
Cooking time: 30-45 minutes

MENU PLANNING TIPS

This granola has a great taste and contains no oil. So now you can eat granola and not get all those calories. The nuts and seeds are some of the best sources of the essential fatty acids and mono-unsaturated fat in our diet. Monounsaturated fat has been found to be the best type of fat to prevent heart disease. This cereal is also a great source of fiber, so eat it to your heart's content. Add fresh fruit to top this delicious breakfast cereal and serve with the milk of your choice to get a great breakfast that is perfect for those busy mornings. You can make extra granola and store in the freezer or refrigerator.

CHERYL'S ALMOND GRANOLA

Makes 5 cups
Prep. time: 5 minutes
Cooking time: 25 minutes

MENU PLANNING TIPS

This granola can be made with a small amount of oil, or without any oil. I like the crispy texture the oil gives the granola, but if you're trying to cut your fat to below 20 percent of the calories, delete the oil. The flavor is still the same with the oil-free version. One of my favorite breakfasts is a large bowl full of fresh chopped fruit, sprinkled with 1/2 cup of either of these two granola recipes. You can top with the Tofu Whipped Cream *(p. 122)* or nonfat vanilla yogurt. This is a delicious low-fat breakfast that is sure to satisfy your taste buds and meet the daily nutrient recommendations for breakfast.

4	cups quick oats
3/4	cup toasted wheat germ
1/2	cup almonds, slivered
1/4	cup pecans, coarsely chopped
1/2	cup unsweetened coconut, shredded (optional)
1/2	teaspoon salt
3/4	cup frozen apple juice concentrate
5	tablespoons honey
2	tablespoons canola oil (optional)
1	tablespoon pure vanilla extract
1/4	teaspoon pure almond extract
1/2	cup dried fruit of choice (dates, raisins, apricots, blueberries, etc.), chopped *or* whole

1. In a large mixing bowl, combine the first six ingredients.

2. In a small mixing bowl, combine the liquid ingredients. I use a small whisk to dissolve the honey into the apple juice concentrate.

3. Drizzle the liquid mixture onto the dry granola and mix well to coat all the dry ingredients evenly. Spread uncooked granola onto large baking sheet with sides. Be sure the granola is not more than 1 inch thick so the granola bakes evenly.

4. Bake for 20 minutes, stirring every 5 to 7 minutes. Add the dried fruit and bake an additional 5 minutes. The granola should be crisp and golden. Do not overcook after adding the fruit to prevent the fruit from hardening. Sometimes I soak the dried fruit in hot water for 1 minute and then drain off the water just before adding to granola to keep the dried fruit moist and to blend the flavors better with the granola. Let cool. Store granola in a sealed container in the refrigerator or freezer.

5. Serve the granola with tofu, soy, or nonfat milk and top with additional fresh fruit, if desired. Makes 5 cups.

BREAKFAST SHAKES

PINEAPPLE-BANANA BREAKFAST SHAKE

Serves 4
Prep. time: 5-10 minutes

MENU PLANNING TIPS

You know you should eat breakfast. But what if you can't face solid food so early in the day? Try drinking your morning meal! These shakes are easy to make and easy to consume in the early morning and even taste great for a low-fat evening snack.

2	cups canned crushed pineapple, drained
1 1/2	cups ice cubes
1 1/3	cups Tofu Yogurt *(p. 117)* **or** nonfat yogurt
2	medium bananas, coarsely chopped
1/2	cup apricot nectar
1/4	cup toasted wheat germ
1/4	teaspoon pure vanilla extract (optional)
1	kiwifruit, peeled and sliced

1. In blender, combine the pineapple, ice cubes, yogurt of choice, bananas, apricot nectar, wheat germ, and vanilla extract. Blend until smooth.

2. Serve in tall glasses; garnish with kiwi slices.

PEACH-BERRY-BANANA FRUIT SHAKE

2	cups Tofu Yogurt *(p. 117) or* nonfat vanilla yogurt
2	cups fresh orange juice
1	cup frozen banana slices
1	cup peaches
1/2	cup strawberries, coarsely chopped
1	tablespoon honey
1/2	teaspoon vanilla
2	cups ice cubes

In a blender, combine all ingredients. Blend on high speed until smooth and creamy.

BREAKFAST SCONES WITH FRUIT BUTTER AND FRUIT PLATTER

ALMOND-OAT SCONES

Prep. time: 20 minutes
Cooking time: 20 minutes
Makes 12 Scones

1 1/2	cups unbleached flour
3	tablespoons brown sugar (optional, can replace with 3 tablespoons honey added to liquid ingredients)
2	teaspoons cream of tartar
1	teaspoon baking soda
1/4	teaspoon salt
1 1/3	cups quick oats
1/2	cup canola oil, chilled
1/2	teaspoon almond extract
5	tablespoons almonds, sliced and chopped fine
1/2	cup currants *or* unsweetened coconut, shredded
1/2	cup tofu *or* soy *or* nonfat milk
2	tablespoons additional milk of choice

MENU PLANNING TIPS

These scones combine the flavors of grains, nuts, and fruit to form delicious scones. They are perfect at breakfast with a fresh fruit platter or served with your afternoon tea. The Red Berry Spread or the Peach or Apricot Butter (recipes following) is the perfect topping for these scones.

1. Preheat oven to 375°F. Coat a large baking sheet with nonstick cooking spray.
2. Sift unbleached flour, cream of tartar, baking soda, and salt into mixing bowl. Mix quick oats and brown sugar into the sifted dry ingredients.
3. Combine oil and almond extract. If using honey for the sweetener, whisk it into the oil until it is dissolved.
4. Pour the oil mixture into the dry ingredients and toss with a fork until texture resembles coarse crumbs. Stir in the almonds and currants or coconut. Add 1/2 cup milk; stir to combine and moisten all the flour. Knead a few times to combine the ingredients thoroughly. (Avoid overkneading or the dough will have a tough texture.)
5. Working on a lightly floured board with well-floured hands, pat the dough to a circle about 1/2 inch thick. Using a 2 1/2-inch fluted biscuit cutter, cut rounds from the dough and place them on the prepared baking sheet. Gather the scraps into a ball, pat them out, and cut more scones until all the dough has been used.
6. Place the scones on the baking sheet. Brush the tops of the scones with the remaining 2 teaspoons of milk. Bake for 12 to 15 minutes, or until golden. Transfer the scones to a wire rack. Serve warm or at room temperature. Serve with Red Berry Spread or Peach or Apricot Butter (recipes following).

Makes 12 Scones
Prep. time: 20 minutes
Cooking time: 20 minutes

CURRANT-SESAME SCONES

1⅓	cups unbleached flour
3	tablespoons brown sugar *(optional, can replace with 3 tablespoons honey whipped into oil)*
2	teaspoons cream of tartar
1	teaspoon baking soda
¼	teaspoon salt
3	tablespoons sesame seeds
1⅓	cups oat flour *or* replace with rolled oats blended to a powder
½	cup canola oil, chilled (replaces traditional margarine)
¼	teaspoon pure vanilla extract
½	cup currants
½	cup tofu *or* soy *or* nonfat milk
2	teaspoons additional milk of choice

1. Preheat oven to 375°F. Coat a large baking sheet with nonstick cooking spray.
2. Sift unbleached flour, cream of tartar, baking soda, and salt into mixing bowl.
3. Blend oats to a powder (if oat flour is not available). Add sesame seeds and oat flour to sifted mixture.
4. Combine oil and vanilla extract. If using honey for the sweetener, whisk it into the oil until it is dissolved.
5. Pour the oil mixture into the dry ingredients and toss with a fork until texture resembles coarse crumbs. Stir in the currants. Add ½ cup milk; stir to combine and moisten all the flour. Knead a few times to combine the ingredients thoroughly.
6. Working on a lightly floured board with well-floured hands, pat the dough to a circle about ½ inch thick. Using a 2½-inch fluted biscuit cutter, cut rounds from the dough and place them on the prepared baking sheet. Gather the scraps into a ball, pat them out, and cut more scones until all the dough has been used.
7. Place the scones on the baking sheet. Brush the tops of the scones with the remaining 2 teaspoons of milk.
8. Bake for 12 to 15 minutes, or until golden. Transfer the scones to a wire rack. Serve warm or at room temperature.

RED BERRY SPREAD

1	cup fresh *or* thawed frozen whole strawberries
½	cup fresh *or* thawed frozen raspberries
1	tablespoon honey
2	teaspoons brown sugar (optional)
1	cinnamon stick
1	tablespoon grated lemon peel

1. In a 1-quart saucepan, combine all ingredients. Bring to a boil over medium heat. Reduce the heat to low. Simmer, stirring frequently, for 30 minutes, or until the mixture is thick. Remove and discard the cinnamon stick. If you choose to blend the berries for a smooth spread, it is best to blend before boiling.
2. Cool, then transfer to a bowl or jar. Store, tightly covered, in the refrigerator. Serve with scones.

Makes 1 cup
Prep. time: 5 minutes
Cooking time: 30 minutes

MENU PLANNING TIPS

Red Berry Spread is good with scones, as well as with any other breakfast or brunch bread, pancake, or waffle. Blending the berries before cooking will give you a smooth spread. Cooking the whole berries gives you more of a fresh fruit jam taste. Any fresh fruit can be used in this spread. Be creative; try your favorite fruit combinations. You can also thicken this spread by adding a small amount of cornstarch if you need to speed up the process of thickening, or if you want to use juices in the spread. Add 1 teaspoon cornstarch per cup of liquid used and add to cold liquid before combining with other fruit.

34

PEACH OR APRICOT BUTTER

2   cups dried peaches *or* apricots

1   12-ounce can unsweetened frozen apple juice concentrate, undiluted

1½   cups water

1   teaspoon ground cinnamon (optional)

1. Soak dried peaches or apricots in apple juice concentrate overnight. For last-minute preparation, combine dried fruit and juice concentrate and bring to a boil, then simmer, covered, for approximately 10 minutes, or until fruit is softened. Let cool.

2. Blend softened fruit in blender or food processor until buttery smooth; add cinnamon if desired.

3. Serve with scones, or on toast. This is a very thick, spreadable mixture. This can also be used with waffles or pancakes, served with nondairy whipped topping.

Makes 4 cups
Prep. time: 5 minutes
Cooking time: 10 minutes

FIVE-GRAIN COOKED CEREAL

1   cup whole-grain oats

½   cup cracked wheat

½   cup whole-grain barley

½   cup cornmeal

½   cup millet

6   cups water

1   teaspoon salt

½   cup dried fruit (apricots, dates, raisins, blueberries, etc.)

½   cup tofu *or* soy *or* nonfat milk (optional)

1. Place all the ingredients in the Crock-Pot and cover. Cook on low; slow-cook 6 hours. If longer cooking time is necessary, add more water so the cereal does not dry out too much. If you cook the cereal on high, it can be done as soon as 3 hours. This recipe can be cut in half; just remember to follow the basic guidelines of one part grain to two parts water.

2. Serve with fresh fruit, fruit sauce of choice *(recipes in this breakfast section),* *and/or* nondairy milk or nonfat milk.

Makes 6 cups
Prep. time: 5 minutes
Cooking time: 6 hours or overnight in Crock-Pot

MENU PLANNING TIPS

This is a great way to wake up to breakfast, already cooked. While you are sleeping, the Crock-Pot is slowly cooking these whole grains and releasing the wonderful flavors hidden within them. (Note: Use any combination of whole grains to equal 3 cups.)

QUICK-COOKING SEVEN-GRAIN CEREAL

3½   cups water

¼   teaspoon salt

1¾   cups rolled oats

¼   cup seven-grain cereal (the grains are crushed and sold as a mix)

¼-½ cup dried blueberries, raisins, *or* dates

¼   cup slivered almonds (optional)

½   cup tofu *or* soy *or* nonfat milk

1. Place water and salt in a medium-size pan; cover and bring to a boil.

2. Add oats and seven-grain cereal to boiling water. Return to a boil and then lower temperature and simmer, covered, for 10 minutes. Add dried fruit and nuts during the last 3 to 5 minutes of cooking.

Serves 4
Prep. time: 5 minutes
Cooking time: 10 minutes

MENU PLANNING TIPS

This cereal is a great way to get your fiber and B vitamins. Add milk of choice, and top with fresh fruit or fresh fruit sauce *(p. 37).*

FRESH FRUIT SAUCE

2	cups fresh berries *or* fruit of choice
1/2	teaspoon pure vanilla extract

1. Place one-half of berries or fresh fruit of choice in blender and blend until smooth.
2. Add vanilla extract and chopped fresh fruit to blended fruit and mix well. Serve chilled or at room temperature.

Serves 4
Prep. time:
5-10 minutes

MENU PLANNING TIPS
Serve over pancakes, waffles, or toast.

MUESLI-NUT FRUIT SALAD

FRUIT SALAD:

1/2	cantaloupe, peeled and cut into 1-inch pieces
1	small apple, peeled, cored, and cut into bite-size pieces
1	mango, peeled and cut into chunks
1	banana, thinly sliced
2	peaches, coarsely chopped
5	strawberries, fresh *or* frozen, cut in slices

MUESLI-NUT TOPPING:

1/4	cup quick *or* rolled oats
1/4	cup unsalted cashews, almonds, pecans, *or* walnuts
2-4	tablespoons unsweetened, shredded coconut
1	tablespoon sesame seeds
1/8	teaspoon ground cinnamon
1/2	cup raisins, dried blueberries, *or* dates (optional)
2	cups Tofu Yogurt *(p. 117)* or nonfat yogurt

1. In a medium-size mixing bowl, combine the fruit.
2. In a food processor, combine the oats, nuts, coconut, sesame seeds, and cinnamon. Process with on/off turns until coarsely ground; do not overprocess or the mixture will become a paste. Sprinkle over the fruit.
3. Stir in the raisins, dates, dried blueberries, or dried fruit of choice. Serve topped with yogurt of choice.

Serves 1 or 2
Prep. time: 10 minutes

MENU PLANNING TIPS
This is an easy alternative to breakfast cereals, a great dieter's breakfast. Be sure to eat lots of this so that it will hold you till the next meal. Serve in a large salad bowl; it's a great way to eat a huge, satisfying breakfast and not feel guilty. You can use your favorite combination of fruit. This recipe is my favorite combination and the amount I eat almost every day for breakfast. I top my fruit with either this nut mixture, or I'll use one of the granolas from the breakfast section. Surprisingly, you'll find this will satisfy you for many hours.

Lunch

SANDWICHES

Grilled Vegetable Sandwich With
Creamy Herb Dressing

Roasted Vegetable Pitas With
Creamy Herb Dressing

Lentil Patties in Pita Pockets With
Creamy Cucumber Dressing

Italian-Style Vegetarian Hoagie

Oven-baked Seasoned Fries

Guilt-free Burgers

Toasted Bagels With Roasted Red
Pepper Spread

Garbanzo Bean Sandwiches

Mexican Chili Burgers

Oven-baked Mexi-Fries

GRILLED VEGETABLE SANDWICH WITH CREAMY HERB DRESSING

2 medium zucchini, cut lengthwise into ¼-inch oblong slices

1 medium red bell pepper, cut into 1-inch pieces

1 medium yellow bell pepper, cut into 1-inch pieces (optional)

1 large onion, cut into ½-inch slices

½ cup sun-dried tomatoes, soaked for 2 minutes in boiling water and chopped

2 garlic cloves, thinly sliced (optional)

4 6- to 8-inch sections of French bread

MARINADE:

¼ cup lemon juice

2 tablespoons olive oil

1-2 teaspoons light molasses (can substitute honey or sugar)

1 tablespoon fresh basil, chopped *or* 1 teaspoon dried basil

1 tablespoon fresh thyme *or* ½ teaspoon dried thyme (optional)

¼ teaspoon salt (optional)

1. Prepare Creamy Herb Dressing *(p. 124)* and refrigerate until serving time.

2. Prepare and cut vegetables. Rehydrate sun-dried tomatoes as directed in ingredient list.

3. Mix together all marinade ingredients.

4. In large bowl, toss together vegetables and marinade. If desired, you can let the vegetable mixture marinate for 2 hours in the refrigerator in a zip-top plastic bag, but this step is not necessary.

5. Grill or roast following these directions:

GRILLING:

Place vegetables in a wire grilling basket, coated with cooking spray. Prepare grill. Place grilling basket on grill rack; grill 5 minutes, basting occasionally with remaining marinade. Turn basket over; grill 2 minutes, basting occasionally. Cut the bread horizontally and brush with 3 tablespoons of the marinade. Place bread, cut side down, on grill rack and grill with the vegetables an additional 3 minutes, or until vegetables are tender and bread is toasted.

ROASTING OR BROILING:

Preheat oven to broil. Place vegetable mixture on a baking sheet and spread out thinly. Broil for 5 minutes; turn vegetable mixture and baste with more marinade if needed. Broil for an additional 5 minutes, or until vegetables are just tender and roasted. Remove vegetable mixture from the oven and put the bread, brushed with 3 tablespoons of marinade, under the broiler, toasting until lightly browned.

6. Spread Creamy Herb Dressing liberally on toasted sides of both pieces of bread. Top bottom piece with liberal amount of grilled or roasted vegetable mixture; top with other half of bread. Serve with side dish of creamy dressing for dipping and extra drizzling.

Serves 4
Prep. time: 10 minutes
Cooking time: 10 minutes

MENU PLANNING TIPS

This sandwich can be grilled or roasted. Directions are included for both techniques. The vegetable mixture makes a delicious full-meal sandwich, and the Creamy Herb Dressing enhances its flavor. Be sure the dressing isn't too thick, or it will overpower the taste of the vegetables. The consistency of French dressing is about right. A baked potato chip tastes great on the side of this sandwich and still maintains the theme of this low-fat, healthy menu. For dessert, add a fat-free sorbet purchased from the grocery store, or try a cool, refreshing fruit smoothie or sorbet from the dessert section of this book.

ROASTED VEGETABLE PITAS WITH CREAMY HERB DRESSING

1	cup yellow summer squash, cut in ½-inch diagonal slices
1	red pepper, cut into wedges
1	small onion, cut into eight wedges
2	garlic cloves, thinly sliced
1	large tomato, cut into eight wedges
½	cup spinach leaves, washed and torn into bite-size pieces (optional)
1½	teaspoons olive oil
1½	teaspoons fresh oregano, chopped, *or* ½ teaspoon dried oregano
1½	teaspoons fresh basil, chopped, *or* ½ teaspoon dried basil (optional)
¼	teaspoon salt (optional)
⅓	cup Creamy Herb Dressing *(p. 124)*
2-4	whole-wheat pita pocket halves

1. Prepare and cut vegetables.

2. Combine in mixing bowl all the above ingredients except the tomatoes and creamy dressing. Toss vegetable mixture to lightly glaze the vegetables with olive oil and herbs.

3. Spoon vegetable mixture onto a broiler pan or cookie sheet coated with nonstick cooking spray. Broil 5 minutes; add tomatoes and spinach leaves to vegetable mixture and stir. Baste with additional marinade and broil for 5 additional minutes, or until vegetables are just tender and lightly browned. Tomatoes and spinach should be just warmed; if you prefer the tomato softer, add with vegetable mixture at the beginning of the 10 minutes.

4. Prepare the Creamy Herb Dressing while the vegetables are broiling.

5. Divide vegetable mixture evenly between two pita halves. Drizzle 2 tablespoons creamy dressing over each pita sandwich. Serve.

Serves 2
Prep. time: 10 minutes
Cooking time: 10 minutes

MENU PLANNING TIPS

You can use eggplant, zucchini, and red, green, or yellow pepper in this vegetable mixture. Serve with baked potato wedges.

LENTIL PATTIES IN PITA POCKETS WITH CREAMY CUCUMBER DRESSING

Serves 6-8
Prep. time: 15 minutes
Cooking time: 30 minutes

MENU PLANNING TIPS

These delicious lentil patties have a unique flavor, similar to the seasoning in a falafel. I like to make these patties with leftover lentils from lentil soup or leftover rice. This saves time in preparation and is a good way to use leftovers creatively. Serve these patties in the pita pockets, or serve with rice or potatoes for a main meal. Any way you serve them, they are sure to be enjoyed by all. Garnish with chopped tomatoes or red peppers. Serve with carrots and celery sticks on the side.

6-8	whole-wheat pita pocket halves
1	cup Creamy Cucumber Dressing *(p. 124)*
16-24	Lentil Patties, 1½-inch diameter

1. Prepare Lentil Patties (recipe following).
2. Crumble Lentil Patties into pita pocket halves.
3. Top each pita pocket sandwich with 2 tablespoons Creamy Cucumber Dressing. Serve with side dish of dressing for extra drizzling.

LENTIL PATTIES

1¼	cups uncooked lentils *or* 3 cups cooked lentils
1	small onion, chopped
½	cup tofu, soft, *or* four egg whites
2	garlic cloves, minced
½	teaspoon ground cumin
1	teaspoon sage
1	teaspoon garlic powder
¼	teaspoon salt
⅛	teaspoon hot sauce (optional)
1	cup whole-grain rice, cooked
1	small carrot, shredded
½	cup cracker crumbs
½	cup pecans, chopped (optional, for texture)

1. Place lentils in 2-quart saucepan. Cover with water and bring to a boil over medium-high heat. Reduce heat to low. Simmer, covered, for 30 minutes or until lentils are tender; drain.
2. Line baking sheet with a double thickness of paper towels. Spoon cooked lentils onto the paper towels. Let stand about 20 minutes, or until lentils are cool and most of moisture has been absorbed.
3. In blender, combine half the cooked, drained lentils, onion, tofu or egg whites, garlic cloves, cumin, sage, garlic powder, salt, and hot sauce and blend until smooth. Mixture will be thick.
4. Place blended lentil mixture in mixing bowl and add rice, shredded carrots, cracker crumbs, and chopped pecans. Mix thoroughly. Add more cracker crumbs, if needed, to thicken patties.
5. Coat bottom of large skillet with small amount of canola oil or nonstick cooking spray. Place 2 rounded tablespoons full of lentil mixture in palm of hand; shape into patty. Repeat with remaining lentil mixture.
6. Place patties in skillet. Flatten to even thickness with spatula. Cook patties over medium heat for 6 to 7 minutes on each side until browned on both sides.

TALIAN-STYLE VEGETARIAN HOAGIE

1	18- to 24-inch hoagie roll *(French bread also can be used for this)*
2½	tablespoons light olive oil
1-2	teaspoons dried oregano
	garlic powder to taste
	salt to taste (optional)
8	ounces Worthington Meatless Corned Beef *and/or* Smoked Turkey (optional)
2-3	large tomatoes, sliced thick
2	cucumbers, peeled and sliced lengthwise
4-5	cups head lettuce, shredded
1	large sweet red pepper, sliced thin
½	sweet onion, sliced in thin circles (optional)

1. Preheat oven to broil if toasting the bread. Cut the hoagie roll lengthwise and open it for assembly. Drizzle olive oil over both sides of bread, and then place top piece over bottom piece and lightly squeeze together to help evenly absorb the olive oil. Open roll with oiled sides up and sprinkle oregano, garlic powder, and salt over oil layer. Toast bread under broiler for 2 to 4 minutes, if you desire toasted bread.

2. Fold meatless corned beef and/or turkey slices in half and line bottom piece of the roll. Top with tomato slices, cucumbers, lettuce, sweet red peppers, and onions.

3. Drizzle vegetable layer with more olive oil and sprinkle with oregano, garlic powder, and salt, if desired. You can also use a low-fat Italian dressing to drizzle over vegetable mixture. Cover with top half of bread, cut (if using the long loaves), and serve.

OVEN-BAKED SEASONED FRIES

1½	pounds *or* seven medium baking potatoes, peeled and cut into thin strips
1	tablespoon canola *or* light olive oil
½	teaspoon garlic powder
¼-½	teaspoon paprika (optional)
¼	teaspoon salt (optional)

1. Preheat oven to 450°F.

2. Combine all ingredients in a bowl; toss well. Arrange the potatoes in a single layer on a baking sheet. Bake for 15 to 20 minutes, or until golden brown.

Serves 4
Prep. time: 10 minutes
Cook time: 5 minutes

MENU PLANNING TIPS
This Italian hoagie is perfect for a fast dinner, a quick-to-prepare picnic, or a party. I find it faster to assemble one long hoagie, versus making four separate ones, but you can assemble this great Italian filling into individual rolls or long rolls. Some bakeries make whole-wheat hoagie rolls, which increases your fiber intake for the day. You can enjoy the hoagie toasted or left cold. Either way, this hearty sandwich will be a hit. The oregano and olive oil seasoning give this vegetarian hoagie the Italian touch.

Serves 4
Prep. time: 10 minutes
Baking time: 15-20 minutes

MENU PLANNING TIPS
Serve these garlic-flavored oven fries with the Guilt-free Burger and any other vegetable dish. They add a unique twist to the traditional baked potato and have a quicker baking time. Be sure to use baking potatoes. Thin-skinned potatoes, which have a higher sugar content than baking potatoes, will burn on the outside before the inside is cooked, resulting in a soggy fry.

GUILT-FREE BURGERS

Makes 16 three-inch burgers
Prep. time: 15 minutes
Cooking time: 15 minutes

MENU PLANNING TIPS

Serve these delicious burger sandwiches on whole-wheat burger buns with Ranch Soy Mayonnaise *(p. 123)* or other dressing of choice, tomato slices, lettuce, and sliced onion. You can vary the flavor by adding different vegetables and dressings. Add Oven-Baked Seasoned Fries *(p. 43)* or baked potato chips for a light lunch or dinner.

1½	cups water
1	cup seven-grain cereal
¼	cup water
1	teaspoon McKay's Chicken-Style Seasoning *or* Chicken-like Seasoning *(p. 121)*
½	cup onions, chopped
½	cup carrots, shredded
½	cup zucchini, shredded (optional)
1	teaspoon dried thyme
2	cups cooked brown rice
10	ounces soft tofu *or* ½ cup egg whites *or* egg substitute
2-4	slices whole-wheat toast, crushed into crumbs *or* ½-1 cup cracker crumbs
¼	cup walnuts, chopped
1½	teaspoons garlic powder
1-2	teaspoons sage

1. In a small microwaveable bowl, combine 1½ cups of water with the seven-grain cereal. Cover and cook on high for 5 minutes. Grains should be softened. Let sit to cool while preparing the remaining ingredients.

2. In a large nonstick skillet over medium heat, stir together and heat the water and McKay's Chicken-Style Seasoning or Chicken-like Seasoning. Add the onions, carrots, zucchini, and thyme; cook, stirring frequently, for 4 to 5 minutes, or until the vegetables are tender and the liquid has evaporated.

3. In large mixing bowl, mix together the sautéed vegetables, softened grains, rice, tofu or egg whites, toasted bread crumbs, walnuts, garlic powder, and sage. Mix well. If mixture is too thin to form patties, add one to two slices of bread, crushed into crumbs, to thicken pattie mixture.

4. Shape into 3-inch diameter patties that are ½ to 1 inch in thickness.

5. Wash and dry the nonstick skillet. Spray with nonstick cooking spray and place it over medium heat. Add the patties and sauté for about 5 minutes per side, or until golden.

TOASTED BAGELS WITH ROASTED RED PEPPER SPREAD

8	ounces soft tofu, well drained and squeezed dry between paper towels
1	tablespoon tofu *or* soy *or* nonfat milk
1	tablespoon lemon juice
1	teaspoon honey
1/8	teaspoon salt
1/4	cup roasted sweet red peppers, chopped
1/4	cup cucumber, seeds removed, grated
2	tablespoons green onion, chopped
4	bagels, split in half
8	large tomato slices

1. Crumble the tofu into a food processor. Add the milk, lemon juice, honey and salt; process until smooth. Transfer to a small bowl.

2. Stir in the red peppers, cucumbers, and green onions. Cover and refrigerate for at least 1 hour.

3. To serve, toast the bagels. Spread with the red pepper-tofu mixture; top each half with a tomato slice.

Serves 4
Prep. time: 10 minutes
Cooking time: 5 minutes

MENU PLANNING TIPS
This toasted bagel makes a nice light lunch or dinner, and even works for breakfast.

GARBANZO BEAN SANDWICHES

1	can garbanzo beans (15-16 ounces), rinsed and drained
1/2	cup water
2	tablespoons fresh parsley, chopped
2	tablespoons walnuts, chopped
1	tablespoon onion, finely chopped
1	clove garlic, finely chopped
4	whole-wheat pita breads (6 inches in diameter)
	lettuce leaves
1	medium tomato, seeded and chopped (3/4 cup)
1/2	medium cucumber, sliced and cut into fourths
1/2	cup Creamy Cucumber Dressing *(p. 124) or* purchased creamy cucumber dressing

1. Place beans, water, parsley, walnuts, onion, and garlic in food processor or blender. Cover and process until smooth.

2. Cut each pita bread in half to form two pockets; line with lettuce leaves. Spoon sandwich filling into each pita half. Add tomato, cucumber, and dressing. Serve.

Serves 4
Prep. time: 10 minutes

MENU PLANNING TIPS
This is a great lunch box idea. Put the dressing in a small sealed container and drizzle over the sandwich filling just before eating.

MEXICAN CHILI BURGERS

1½	cups water
1	cup seven-grain cereal
10	ounces soft tofu, blended, *or* ½ cup egg whites *or* egg substitute
1-2	teaspoons McKay's Chicken-Style Seasoning *or* Chicken-like Seasoning *(p. 121)*
¼	cup fresh cilantro, minced
2-3	teaspoons canned green chilies, chopped
1½	teaspoons dried oregano
1½	teaspoons cumin
1	teaspoon chili powder
2	teaspoons garlic powder
1	cup onions, chopped fine
½	cup carrots, shredded
2	cups cooked brown rice
½-1	cup cracker crumbs
1	cup plum tomatoes, seeded and chopped

1. In a small microwaveable bowl, combine 1½ cups of water with the seven-grain cereal, cover, and cook on high for 5 minutes. Grains should be softened. Let sit to cool while preparing the remaining ingredients.
2. In blender container, blend the soft tofu to the consistency of soft cottage cheese. If tofu is too thick, add a small amount of water. If using the egg whites, slightly beat them.
3. In large mixing bowl, pour blended tofu or beaten eggs and add McKay's Chicken-Style Seasoning or Chicken-like Seasoning, cilantro, green chilies, oregano, cumin, chili powder, and garlic powder. Mix well. Add the onions, carrots, rice, cracker crumbs, tomatoes, and softened grain mixture. Mix well. If mixture is too thin to form burgers, add additional cracker crumbs. If mixture is too crumbly, add a few tablespoons of water to hold mixture together.
4. Shape into patties that are 4 inches in diameter and ½ inch in thickness.
5. Spray nonstick skillet with nonstick cooking spray and place over medium heat. Add the patties and sauté for about 5 minutes per side, or until golden brown.

OVEN-BAKED MEXI-FRIES

1½	pounds *or* seven medium baking potatoes, peeled and cut into thin strips
1	tablespoon canola *or* light olive oil
2	teaspoons chili powder
½	teaspoon salt (optional)
½	teaspoon dried oregano
¼	teaspoon garlic powder
¼	teaspoon ground cumin

1. Preheat oven to 450°F.
2. Combine all ingredients in a bowl; toss well. Arrange potatoes in a single layer on a baking sheet. Bake for 15 to 20 minutes, or until golden brown.

Makes 12 four-inch burgers, ½ inch thick
Prep. time: 10 minutes
Cooking time: 15-20 minutes

MENU PLANNING TIPS
Serve this great-tasting Mexican Chili Burger on whole-wheat burger buns spread with Tofu Sour Cream *(p. 122)* or fat-free sour cream. Add chopped green leaf lettuce. Guacamole and salsa add the final touch. Accompany burgers with the Oven-baked Mexi-Fries (recipe following) to add a unique taste. These burgers taste great in an open-faced sandwich. Just leave off the top half.

Serves 4
Prep. time: 10 minutes
Baking time: 15-20 minutes

Lunch Salads

SALADS

Waldorf Potato Salad

Waldorf Potato Salad Dressing

Summer Harvest Chicken-
Potato Salad

Soy Ranch Dressing

Caesar Salad

Freshly Made Croutons

Italian Spice Blend

Caesar Salad Dressing

Haystacks

Garden Greek Salad

Greek Salad Dressing

WALDORF POTATO SALAD

8	thin-skinned potatoes, peeled and chopped in large pieces
1	cup Waldorf Potato Salad Dressing (recipe following)
4	Golden Delicious apples, cored, peeled, and chopped
1	cup celery, chopped
½	cup red grapes, cut in half
¼-½	cup walnuts (optional)

1. Prepare and cook potatoes.
2. Prepare Waldorf Potato Salad Dressing.
3. In mixing bowl, combine potatoes, apples, celery, grapes, walnuts (optional); mix well.
4. Toss dressing over potato-apple mixture, evenly coating all ingredients with dressing.
5. Chill until serving time.

Serves 12
Prep. time: 10 minutes
Cooking time: 20 minutes

MENU PLANNING TIPS

This makes a great side dish to any meal. The combination of apples and potatoes may sound different, but you'll be pleasantly surprised at the great flavor when you try it.

WALDORF POTATO SALAD DRESSING

1	cup water
½	cup Soyagen (soy milk powder)
1	pinch salt
2	tablespoons sugar *or* honey
2-3	tablespoons Hidden Valley Ranch dressing mix, to taste
½	cup light olive oil *or* canola oil
	juice of two large limes

In blender, place water, Soyagen,* salt, honey or sugar, and ranch dressing mix and process until smooth. While blending, slowly pour oil into mixture. Mixture will thicken. Pour mixture out into container. Stir in fresh lime juice.

Makes 2 cups

If you do not have access to Soyagen, a soy milk powder, do not use any other soy or tofu milk powder; it will not thicken. It is best to replace the water and Soyagen with 10 ounces tofu, blended with enough water to thin to white-sauce consistency.

SUMMER HARVEST CHICKEN-POTATO SALAD

SUMMER HARVEST CHICKEN-POTATO SALAD

8   small red potatoes with skins, halved

2   cups green beans, fresh *or* frozen, trimmed and cut into 1-inch pieces

1   12.5-ounce can low-fat Worthington FriChik, each piece cut into 3 strips, then halved

2   cups celery, thinly sliced

1/2 sweet red pepper, sliced and chopped

1   cup Soy Ranch Dressing (recipe following)
    or

1   cup Yogurt Ranch Dressing:

   1/2 cup nonfat plain yogurt

   1/3 cup purchased fat-free ranch salad dressing

   torn salad greens for bed of lettuce

Serves 4-6
Prep. time: 15 minutes
Cooking time: 20 minutes

MENU PLANNING TIPS
Make a meal with this Summer Harvest Chicken-Potato Salad. Accompany it with some whole-grain rolls or bread.

1. In large saucepan, add small amount of water to the potatoes and steam until potatoes are just tender. Remove potatoes from pan with a slotted spoon, and cool. Add green beans to pan with potato water and cook an additional 5 to 7 minutes, or until green beans are just tender. Drain; rinse briefly with cold water to stop additional cooking. Place in large serving bowl.

2. Add FriChik, celery, and red pepper.

3. If using Soy Ranch Dressing, see the recipe following. If using the Yogurt Ranch Dressing, combine ingredients in a small bowl and blend well.

4. Pour dressing of choice over salad; toss gently. Serve immediately on plates lined with salad greens, or refrigerate until serving time.

SOY RANCH DRESSING

1   cup water

2/3 cup Soyagen (soy milk powder)

1   pinch salt

1   tablespoon sugar *or* honey

4   tablespoons Hidden Valley Ranch dressing mix

1/4 teaspoon garlic powder

1/4 teaspoon onion powder

1/2 cup light olive oil *or* canola oil

   juice of two large limes *or* one lemon

Makes 2 cups

1. In blender, place water, Soyagen,* salt, honey or sugar, ranch dressing mix, garlic powder, and onion powder and process until smooth. While blending, slowly pour oil into mixture. Mixture will thicken. Pour mixture into a container.

2. Stir in fresh lime or lemon juice. Dressing should thicken more with the addition of lime or lemon juice. Chill in sealed container until serving.

If you do not have access to Soyagen, a soy milk powder, do not use any other soy or tofu milk powder; it will not thicken. It is best to replace the water and Soyagen with 2/3 cup tofu, blended with enough water to thin to white-sauce consistency.

Serves 12
Prep. time: 10 minutes
Cooking time: 5 minutes

MENU PLANNING TIPS

This is a low-fat version of the traditional Caesar salad that contains fresh garlic, anchovies, eggs, and lots of olive oil. This entrée-size salad contains no eggs, no anchovies, and much less olive oil. It has a garlic-flavored cream sauce that gives a delicious light taste. The freshly made seasoned croutons add the final topping to this great salad.

CAESAR SALAD

1	12.5-ounce can Worthington FriChik (optional), drained, cut into strips
or 1	10-ounce package firm tofu, cut into 1-inch cubes
½	teaspoon Italian Spice Blend (recipe following)
¼	teaspoon garlic powder
¼	teaspoon McKay's Chicken-Style Seasoning *or* Chicken-like Seasoning *(p. 121)*
6	cups Romaine lettuce, torn into bite-size pieces
3	cups green leaf lettuce *or* spinach leaves, torn into bite-size pieces
1	carrot, peeled and grated
2	cups Freshly Made Croutons (recipe following)
	Caesar Salad Dressing *(p. 53)*
	freshly-grated Parmesan cheese or Cheeseless "Parmesan" Cheese *(p. 127)*

1. Drain FriChik or tofu; cut FriChik into strips or tofu into cubes. In bowl, combine FriChik or tofu, Italian Spice Blend, garlic powder, and McKay's Chicken-Style Seasoning or Chicken-like Seasoning and toss well. Coat nonstick skillet with non-stick cooking spray; place over medium-high heat until hot. Add seasoned FriChik or tofu; cook 4 minutes on each side, or until browned. Remove from skillet; let cool.

2. Combine lettuce, carrots, 1½ cups of the croutons, and seasoned FriChik or tofu in a large bowl; toss well. Drizzle dressing over Caesar salad mixture; toss well to coat evenly.

3. Place 2 cups of salad on each of four salad plates. Top with remaining ½ cup croutons. Freshly grated Parmesan cheese or Cheeseless "Parmesan" Cheese can be lightly sprinkled over salad, if desired.

FRESHLY MADE CROUTONS

2	cups (about 4 slices) whole-wheat bread, cut into 1-inch cubes
	olive oil-flavored nonstick cooking spray
1	teaspoon Italian Spice Blend (recipe following)
¼	teaspoon garlic powder
	dash salt (optional)

1. Preheat oven to 350°F.

2. Arrange bread cubes in a single layer on baking sheet. Lightly coat bread cubes with cooking spray and sprinkle with Italian Spice Blend (recipe following), garlic powder, and salt to taste. Toss well. Rearrange seasoned bread cubes in single layer. Bake at 350°F for 15 minutes, or until lightly browned; set aside.

ITALIAN SPICE BLEND

2	tablespoons fresh oregano, chopped, *or* 2 teaspoons dried oregano
1	tablespoon fresh basil, chopped, *or* 1 teaspoon dried basil
1	tablespoon fresh mint, *or* 1 teaspoon dried mint
½	teaspoon rubbed sage
1	teaspoon granulated garlic
½	teaspoon onion powder

Place all ingredients in a clean spice or coffee grinder; process until finely ground. Store in an airtight container.

CAESAR SALAD DRESSING

Prep. time:
5 minutes/tofu option
Overnight /yogurt option

1	recipe tofu *or* yogurt cheese *(option recipes below)*
2-3	tablespoons water
1	teaspoon dry mustard
1½	teaspoons fresh lemon juice (replacement for balsamic vinegar)
1-2	garlic cloves, minced (depending on your love of garlic)

Combine tofu or yogurt option with water, dry mustard, lemon juice, and garlic in blender or food processor; process well. Set dressing aside. Dressing should be thin. If needed, add additional water to thin the sauce. (Try adding ½ to 1 teaspoon Italian Spice Blend *[p. 52]* to this dressing for variety.)

TOFU OPTION:

1	cup soft tofu
2	tablespoons vegetable oil
1	tablespoon lemon juice
1½	teaspoons honey
½	teaspoon salt

Combine ingredients and blend until smooth.

YOGURT CHEESE OPTION:

8	ounces plain nonfat yogurt

Place colander in a medium bowl. Line colander with four layers of cheesecloth, allowing cheesecloth to extend over outside of edges. Spoon yogurt into colander. Cover loosely with plastic wrap; refrigerate 12 hours. Discard liquid.

HAYSTACKS

Serves 1
Prep time: 10 minutes
Cooking time: 10 minutes

½	cup cooked pinto beans *or* small red beans
2	tablespoons green chilies
¼	teaspoon garlic powder
¼	teaspoon cumin
¼	teaspoon chili powder (more or less, depending on how spicy you like your beans)
1	cup low-fat tortilla chips
1	cup head lettuce, shredded
1	small Roma tomato, chopped
¼	cup carrots, grated
1	tablespoon green onions, sliced (optional)
1	tablespoon black olives, sliced (optional)
2	tablespoons Guacamole *(p. 126)*
2	tablespoons low-fat sour cream *or* Tofu Sour Cream *(p. 122)*
2	tablespoons Thick and Chunky Salsa *(p. 125)*

1. In small saucepan, combine beans, green chilies, garlic powder, cumin, and chili powder and cook over medium heat until heated thoroughly.

2. Place chips on serving plate. Spoon the warm chili bean mixture over the chips. Top the bean mixture with lettuce, tomato, carrots, guacamole, sour cream, and salsa. Serve immediately.

MENU PLANNING TIPS

Haystacks are a regular weekly menu item for many vegetarians. You can make them many ways. Changing the beans, chips, and toppings totally changes the taste. The goal is to keep the combination tasty and moist. The salsa, guacamole, and sour cream add the final touch.

GARDEN GREEK SALAD

1	cup pasta bows
1/4	cup Greek Salad Dressing (recipe following)
4	cups Romaine lettuce, torn into bite-size pieces
1/2	cup carrots, grated
1/2	green pepper, thinly sliced, **and/or** sweet red pepper
1/4	cup artichoke hearts, not marinated
1/4	cup black olives, sliced
1	teaspoon feta cheese (optional)

1. Cook pasta until just tender and drain.
2. Prepare the Greek Salad Dressing and chill until serving time.
3. Prepare and toss together lettuce, carrots, green peppers, artichoke hearts, and black olives. Add cooked pasta and toss. Toss dressing over the entire vegetable/pasta mixture. Place in serving bowl and garnish with feta cheese, if desired.

Serves 6
Prep. time: 10 minutes
Cooking time: 10 minutes

MENU PLANNING TIPS

This is one of my favorite main dish salads. Serve this with garlic bread and enjoy the feast. The pasta added to the lettuce is an interesting twist. It gives this salad a hearty feel, and you'll never miss the feta cheese traditionally served with Greek salad, if you opt not to use cheese.

GREEK SALAD DRESSING

1/3	cup fresh lemon juice
4	tablespoons light olive oil
1/2	teaspoon honey **or** pinch sugar
2	tablespoons green onion, sliced thin (optional)
1	tablespoon fresh oregano **or** 1 teaspoon dried oregano
1/4	teaspoon salt (optional)
2	garlic cloves, minced

1. Mix all dressing ingredients in a container that can be shaken. Shake well until oil and lemon juice have a creamy appearance. Chill until serving. Shake before serving each time.

Makes 1/2 cup

Lunch Soups

SOUPS

Vegetable Split-Pea Soup

Chilled Minted Pea Soup

Chilled Chunky Gazpacho

Creamy Broccoli-Rice Soup

Vegetable Chili

Creamy Garlic Potato Soup

Italian Vegetable Soup

VEGETABLE SPLIT-PEA SOUP

2	quarts water
2	cups dried green split peas
1	stalk celery, coarsely chopped
1	large carrot, chopped
1	small onion, chopped
1/4	teaspoon ground thyme
1	whole bay leaf
	salt to taste
1	package golden George Washington Broth *or* 1 teaspoon McKay's Chicken-Style Seasoning

1. Rinse peas thoroughly in fine strainer under cold water, picking out debris and any blemished peas. Prepare vegetables as directed.

2. In large pan, combine all the above prepared ingredients and bring to a boil for 20 minutes. Cover and let simmer additional 30 minutes. Remove bay leaf before serving.

CHILLED MINTED PEA SOUP

1	cup dried green split peas
1	carrot, peeled and sliced
1/2	cup onion, chopped
1/2	cup celery, chopped
2	tablespoons light olive oil
4	cups water
4	teaspoons McKay's Chicken-Style Seasoning *or* Chicken-like Seasoning *(p. 121)*
2	tablespoons fresh mint leaves, chopped, *or* 2 teaspoons dried mint leaves
1	teaspoon sugar or honey
	salt to taste (optional)
1	cup Tofu Sour Cream *(p. 122)* or nonfat sour cream

1. Rinse peas thoroughly in fine strainer under cold running water, picking out debris and any blemished peas. Set aside.

2. Prepare carrot, onions, and celery.

3. In medium saucepan over medium heat, add oil, carrot, onions, and celery. Cook 5 minutes, or until vegetables are tender, stirring occasionally.

4. Stir in water and McKay's Chicken-Style Seasoning or Chicken-like Seasoning, peas, and 1 tablespoon fresh mint or 1 teaspoon dried mint. Bring to a boil over medium-high heat. Reduce to low; simmer, covered, 1 hour, or until peas are very tender.

5. Place soup in food processor. Add remaining mint, sugar or honey, and salt to taste. Process until smooth, scraping side of bowl occasionally.

6. Place soup in medium bowl; stir in Tofu Sour Cream or nonfat sour cream. Cover tightly with plastic wrap. Refrigerate 3 to 4 hours until well chilled. Garnish with nonfat sour cream or Tofu Sour Cream and fresh mint leaves, if desired.

Serves 8-12
Prep. time: 10 minutes
Cooking time: 1 hour

MENU PLANNING TIPS

This wonderful split-pea soup meal is completed by serving with a tossed green salad and whole-grain rolls. The soup can be slow cooked in a Crock-Pot, ready for dinner when you get home.

Serves 4-6
Prep. time: 20 minutes
Cooking time: 45 minutes

MENU PLANNING TIPS

This soup makes a great appetizer or chilled soup for dinner on a hot summer day.

CHILLED CHUNKY GAZPACHO

Serves 8
Prep. time: 15 minutes

MENU PLANNING TIPS
Cool gazpacho is now an American classic. It makes a great summer soup served with toasted crackers or garlic bread to top off the light meal.

6	cups tomatoes, coarsely chopped *(about 3 pounds)*
1	32-ounce bottle low-sodium tomato juice
2	cups cucumber, peeled and chopped *(about 2 medium)*
1½	cups green bell pepper, chopped
1½	cups Vidalia *or* sweet onion, finely chopped
1	cup celery, chopped
1	tablespoon olive oil
3	tablespoons lemon juice
½	teaspoon salt
½	teaspoon hot sauce
3	garlic cloves, minced

Combine all ingredients in a large bowl; stir well. Cover and chill. Serving size is 1½ cups.

CREAMY BROCCOLI-RICE SOUP

Serves 4
Prep. time: 10 minutes
Cooking time: 20 minutes

MENU PLANNING TIPS
The secret to making this creamy soup without cream is the puréeing of the vegetable mixture in a blender or food processor. Add a tossed salad or raw vegetable sticks and whole grain bread for a light, low-fat meal.

⅓	cup water
3	cups broccoli florets
½	cup chopped onion
3½	cups water
4	teaspoons McKay's Chicken-Style Seasoning *or* Chicken-like Seasoning *(p. 121)*
½	cup uncooked brown or regular white rice
1	cup tofu *or* soy *or* nonfat milk
1	teaspoon fresh oregano leaves *or* ¼ teaspoon dried oregano leaves
½	teaspoon salt (optional)

1. Heat ⅓ cup of water to boiling in 3-quart saucepan over medium heat. Add broccoli and onion. Boil uncovered 6 to 8 minutes, or until almost tender; drain and set aside.

2. Heat 3½ cups water, McKay's Chicken-Style Seasoning or Chicken-like Seasoning, and rice to boiling; reduce heat. Cover and simmer 18 to 20 minutes, or until rice is tender. Place half the broccoli mixture and half the rice mixture in food processor or blender. Cover and process until smooth; return to saucepan. Repeat with remaining broccoli and rice mixtures; return to saucepan. Stir in remaining ingredients; heat through. Serve.

VEGETABLE CHILI

Serves 8
Prep. time: 10 minutes
Cooking time: 15-20 minutes

2	medium potatoes, cubed (2 cups)
1	medium onion, chopped (1/2 cup)
1	small yellow, red, *or* green bell pepper, chopped (1/2 cup)
1	tablespoon chili powder
1	teaspoon ground cumin
1	28-ounce can whole tomatoes, undrained
1	15-ounce can garbanzo beans, rinsed and drained
1	15-ounce can black beans, rinsed and drained
1	8-ounce can tomato purée
1/2	teaspoon garlic powder
1	teaspoon lemon juice
1/2	teaspoon sugar *or* honey
1	medium zucchini, cubed (1 cup)

Garnish with the following:

nonfat sour cream or Tofu Sour Cream *(p. 122)*

chopped fresh cilantro *or* parsley, if desired

1. In saucepan, combine all ingredients, except zucchini, sour cream, and cilantro or parsley. Heat to boiling, breaking up tomatoes and stirring occasionally. Reduce heat. Cover and simmer 13 minutes.

2. Stir in zucchini. Cover and simmer 5 to 7 minutes, or until zucchini is tender. Serve with garnishes.

MENU PLANNING TIPS
This vegetable chili can be made with any combination of beans. Add more or less chili powder, depending on preferred taste. Serve this chili with corn bread for a Mexican fiesta.

CREAMY GARLIC POTATO SOUP

Serves 6
Prep. time: 10 minutes
Cooking time: 15 minutes

1	tablespoon light olive oil
1/2	cup onion, chopped
4	garlic cloves, minced *or* sliced thin
4	cups water
4	teaspoons vegetable broth *or* McKay's Chicken-Style Seasoning *or* Chicken-like Seasoning *(p. 121)*
3	cups potatoes, diced
1	cup fat-free sour cream *or* Tofu Sour Cream *(p. 122)*
2	tablespoons fresh dill, chopped, *or* 2 teaspoons dried dill
	salt to taste (optional)

1. In large pot, heat oil over medium-high heat. Add onion and sauté until translucent; add garlic to onions and sauté an additional 2 to 3 minutes.

2. Add water and broth or seasoning mix and bring to boil. Add potatoes and return to boil. Reduce heat to medium and boil gently 10 minutes, or until potatoes are tender.

3. Working with half of mixture at a time, transfer to food processor or blender. Process until puréed. Return to pot. Stir in remaining ingredients. Stir over low heat until heated through. Serve warm. Garnish with fresh dill and/or green onion slices.

MENU PLANNING TIPS
This creamy potato soup features sautéed garlic and fresh dill, which add intense flavor. Serve this soup with a tossed green salad and whole-grain bread or toast.

ITALIAN VEGETABLE SOUP

Serves 8
Prep. time: 10 minutes
Cooking time: 30 minutes

4   cups water

4   teaspoons vegetable broth *or* McKay's Chicken-Style Seasoning *or* Chicken-like Seasoning *(p. 121)*

2   large tomatoes, chopped and seeded (1 cup)

2   medium carrots, sliced (1 cup)

1   medium stalk celery, sliced ($\frac{1}{2}$ cup)

1   medium onion, chopped ($\frac{1}{2}$ cup)

2   garlic cloves, minced

1   tablespoon fresh parsley, chopped

$1\frac{1}{2}$ teaspoons fresh basil, chopped, *or* $\frac{1}{2}$ teaspoon dried basil

$\frac{1}{4}$ teaspoon salt

1   whole bay leaf

$\frac{1}{2}$ cup uncooked macaroni

1   15-ounce can red *or* white kidney beans, rinsed and drained

$\frac{1}{4}$ cup green beans, cut

2   small zucchini, cut into 1-inch slices (2 cups)

1. In large saucepan, heat water, vegetable broth, tomatoes, carrots, celery, onion, garlic, parsley, basil, salt, and bay leaf to boiling. Reduce heat. Cover and simmer 15 minutes.

2. Stir in macaroni, beans, green beans, and zucchini. Heat to boiling. reduce heat. Cover and simmer 10 to 15 minutes, or until macaroni and vegetables are tender. Remove bay leaf. Serve warm.

MENU PLANNING TIPS
You can use any pasta and any beans that you like for this recipe. Serve with hard rolls or garlic bread on the side.

Main Dish Dinners

PASTA

Chili Macaroni

Pasta With Basil and Tomatoes

Vermicelli With Chunky
Vegetable Sauce

Sun-dried Tomato-Red Pepper
Pesto With Pasta

Linguine With Fresh
Tomato Sauce

Fresh Basil Pesto With Pasta

Asparagus "Alfredo" Pasta Bows

Angel Hair Vegetable Toss

Pasta Tossed With Seasoned Olive
Oil and Fresh Basil

Fettuccine Primavera "Alfredo"

Vegetable Lasagna

CHILI MACARONI

1   cup Loma Linda Redi-Burger *or* cubed firm tofu (optional)

1   medium onion, chopped

1   green pepper, chopped

1   14½-ounce can diced tomatoes

½   cup tomato paste

1   cup water

1   4-ounce can diced green chili peppers, drained

2   teaspoons chili powder

½   teaspoon garlic powder

1   teaspoon oregano

1   teaspoon sugar *or* honey

1   tablespoon lemon juice

     salt to taste (optional)

1   15-ounce can kidney beans

1   cup uncooked macaroni

1   cup loose-pack frozen cut green beans, 1 inch long

1.   In large, nonstick skillet over medium heat, cook the burger (if using), onion, and green pepper.

2.   Stir in undrained canned diced tomatoes, tomato paste, water, green chili peppers, chili powder, garlic powder, oregano, sugar or honey, lemon juice, salt, and kidney beans. Bring to a boil.

3.   Stir in uncooked macaroni and green beans. Return to boiling; reduce heat. Simmer, covered, about 15 minutes, or until macaroni and green beans are tender. Serve in bowls.

Serves 8-10
Prep. time: 15 minutes
Cooking time: 15 minutes

MENU PLANNING TIPS
Serve this speedy skillet meal with corn bread on the side. Use Redi-Burger, a vegetarian burger, tofu, or delete burger.

PASTA WITH BASIL AND TOMATOES

8   ounces dried penne pasta

2   tablespoons olive oil

¼   cup fresh Parmesan cheese, finely grated *or* Cheeseless "Parmesan" Cheese *(p. 127)* (optional)

½   cup green onion, chopped

8   Roma tomatoes, cored, seeded, and chopped

1½   cups lightly packed, chopped fresh basil leaves, plus some sprigs

1.   Bring water for pasta to a boil over high heat. Stir in pasta and cook until just tender, about 10 minutes. Drain well; pour into a wide serving bowl. Add 1 tablespoon olive oil and 2 tablespoons Parmesan cheese (optional); mix well and keep warm.

2.   In a 10- to 12-inch nonstick skillet over medium-high heat, stir onions in remaining oil until limp, about 5 minutes. Add tomatoes and stir just until tomatoes are hot, about 2 minutes; stir in chopped basil.

3.   Pour tomato mixture over hot cooked pasta. Garnish with basil sprigs and optional Parmesan cheese.

Serves 5
Prep. time: 10 minutes
Cooking time: 20 minutes

VERMICELLI WITH CHUNKY VEGETABLE SAUCE

Serves 6
Prep. time: 10 minutes
Cooking time: 10 minutes

MENU PLANNING TIPS
This Chunky Vegetable Sauce is the family favorite at our house. Your whole meal is in this pasta dish. Simply add garlic bread, and you're set. Fresh basil and oregano add the flavoring for this wonderful, fresh garden sauce.

3/4	pound dried vermicelli pasta
1	sweet red pepper, chopped
1	medium onion, chopped
2	stalks celery, chopped
2	small zucchini, sliced
3-4	cloves garlic
4	cups canned diced tomatoes
1	6-ounce can tomato paste
	salt to taste (optional)
1	tablespoon sugar *or* honey
1	tablespoon lemon juice
1/4	cup fresh basil leaves *or* 2 tablespoons dried basil
2	tablespoons fresh oregano leaves *or* 2 teaspoons dried oregano

1. Bring water for pasta to a boil over high heat; stir in pasta and cook until just tender, about 5 to 7 minutes. Drain well; pour into a wide serving bowl.

2. In nonstick skillet over medium-high heat, stir red peppers, onion, and celery until tender, about 5 minutes. Add zucchini and garlic; cook until zucchini is tender. Add tomatoes, tomato paste, salt, sugar or honey, and lemon juice. Stir until tomato mixture comes to a boil, about 5 minutes. Add basil and oregano and cook an additional minute.

3. Serve Chunky Vegetable Sauce over pasta.

SUN-DRIED TOMATO-RED PEPPER PESTO WITH PASTA

Serves 4
Prep. time: 10 minutes
Cooking time: 10 minutes

MENU PLANNING TIPS
This is an easy-to-prepare dish that can be made in 20 minutes. Try tossing in whole pine nuts with pasta for texture. Serve with steamed broccoli, tossed green salad, and garlic bread.

8	ounces dried penne pasta *or* pasta of choice
12	sun-dried tomato halves
1/4	cup fresh basil leaves
2	plum tomatoes, coarsely chopped
2-3	garlic cloves
1-2	roasted red peppers, chopped
1/4-1/2	cup pine nuts
	salt to taste (optional)
1/2	teaspoon onion powder
1/2	teaspoon McKay's Chicken-Style Seasoning or Chicken-like Seasoning *(p. 121)*
1/8	cup olive oil

1. Bring water for pasta to a boil over high heat; stir in pasta and cook just until tender, about 15 minutes. Drain well.

2. Rehydrate sun-dried tomato halves by soaking in boiling water for 2 minutes.

3. In blender or food processor, place basil leaves and process until finely chopped, scraping sides as needed. Add rehydrated sun-dried tomatoes, plum tomatoes, garlic cloves, roasted red peppers, pine nuts, salt, onion powder, and McKay's Chicken-Style Seasoning or Chicken-like Seasoning. While machine is running, pour in olive oil. Thin with 2 to 4 tablespoons of hot water, if needed, to toss with pasta.

4. Toss pesto with hot pasta and serve.

INGUINE WITH FRESH TOMATO SAUCE

Serves 6
Prep. time: 10 minutes
Cooking time: 15 minutes

³/₄	pound fresh *or* dried linguine
1	teaspoon olive oil
1	small onion, chopped
2	yellow *or* red bell peppers, chopped
4	cloves garlic, minced
3	pounds Roma tomatoes, cored and coarsely chopped
1	cup lightly packed fresh basil leaves, slivered
	or
1	cup lightly packed fresh spinach leaves, slivered, with 1 tablespoon dried basil
1	tablespoon lemon juice
1	tablespoon sugar *or* honey to taste (optional)
	Parmesan cheese *or* Cheeseless "Parmesan" Cheese *(p. 127)* (optional)
	salt to taste

1. Bring water for pasta to a boil over high heat. Add pasta and cook, uncovered, just until tender, about 8 minutes. Drain well. To serve hot, pour into a wide bowl. To serve cold, immerse pasta in cool water until cold, then drain well and pour into a wide bowl.

2. In a 3- to 4-quart pan over medium heat, add 1 teaspoon olive oil, onion, and two thirds of the peppers. Cook until vegetables are just tender; add the garlic, and cook an additional 2 minutes. Add two thirds of the tomatoes, ½ cup of the slivered basil, lemon juice, and sweetener of choice. Stir often until tomatoes begin to fall apart, about 10 minutes. Use hot, or let cool to room temperature; cover when cool and let stand, up to 6 hours. Stir into hot or cold cooked tomato mixture the remaining one third of the tomatoes, one third of the peppers, and ½ cup of slivered fresh basil or spinach-dried basil mixture.

3. Spoon hot sauce onto hot pasta, or cool sauce onto cool pasta; mix. Garnish with fresh basil sprigs. Add Parmesan cheese or Cheeseless "Parmesan" Cheese and/or salt to taste, if desired; serve.

MENU PLANNING TIPS
This light and refreshing pasta dish can be served hot or cold. Serve with a fresh tossed green salad and whole-grain bread.

FRESH BASIL PESTO WITH PASTA

FRESH BASIL PESTO WITH PASTA

³/₄	pound pasta of choice
¹/₂	cup fresh basil leaves *or* ¹/₂ cup fresh spinach leaves and ¹/₂-1 tablespoon dried basil
¹/₃	cup pine nuts, plus 3 tablespoons
2	cloves garlic
¹/₄	cup olive oil
¹/₂	teaspoon McKay's Chicken-Style Seasoning *or* Chicken-like Seasoning *(p. 121)*
2	tablespoons hot water

1. Bring a large pot of water to a boil. Cook pasta according to package directions while preparing the pesto.

2. Place fresh basil in food processor or blender and process until finely chopped, scraping sides as needed. Add pine nuts and garlic, and process until finely chopped. With machine running, pour in olive oil in a thin stream. Add McKay's Chicken-Style Seasoning or Chicken-like Seasoning and process briefly to combine. Thin with 2 tablespoons hot water.

3. Toss pesto with hot pasta (cooked and drained) and serve.

Serves 4
Prep. time: 10 minutes
Cooking time: 10 minutes

MENU PLANNING TIPS

This light-tasting, basil-flavored pasta is very satisfying. Try adding warm cannellini (white kidney) beans tossed in with the pesto and pasta. Serve with tossed green salad and whole-grain bread. Garnish with whole pine nuts.

ASPARAGUS "ALFREDO" PASTA BOWS

8	ounces fettuccine pasta
1	pound fresh asparagus *or* broccoli
1	tablespoon olive oil
1	cup "Alfredo" sauce *(see Fettuccine Primavera "Alfredo" recipe, p. 69)*

1. Bring water for pasta to a boil over high heat. Add pasta; cook until tender, 8 to 10 minutes. Drain well; pour into a wide serving bowl.

2. Wash asparagus and scrape off scales, using a vegetable peeler. Break off woody bases where spears snap easily; discard bases. Slice asparagus diagonally into 1-inch pieces. Cook in a small amount of boiling water for 3 to 5 minutes, or till crisp-tender. Drain well.

3. Add "Alfredo" sauce and asparagus pieces to pasta and toss well, coating evenly. Serve immediately. Add freshly grated Parmesan cheese, if desired.

Serves 6
Prep. time: 5 minutes
Cooking time: 10 minutes

MENU PLANNING TIPS

This easy-to-prepare "Alfredo" dish can be made with asparagus or broccoli. The pasta bows are tossed with the garlic-flavored, cholesterol-free "Alfredo" sauce. This is so easy to prepare, and, served with a tossed green salad, it makes a very quick-to-prepare dinner.

ANGEL HAIR VEGETABLE TOSS

Serves 4
Prep. time: 15 minutes
Cooking time: 20 minutes

MENU PLANNING TIPS

This pasta dish is very light tasting and is tossed with lots of delicious vegetables. The chili flakes add a zesty flavor but are optional because they can be irritating to some people. Serve this full-meal dish with seasoned garlic toast and enjoy.

³/₄	pound broccoli florets
1	pound carrots, thinly sliced
³/₄	pound fresh *or* dried angel hair pasta
2	cups spinach leaves, whole or sliced
1	cup zucchini, sliced
1	cup mushrooms, sliced
1	cup green onions, sliced
2	garlic cloves, minced
2	cups vegetable *or* vegetarian chicken broth (2 cups hot water mixed with 2 teaspoons vegetable broth mix *or* McKay's Chicken-Style Seasoning *or* Chicken-like Seasoning *(p. 1*
³/₄-1	cup dried tomatoes (not packed in oil), chopped fine
¹/₄	teaspoon hot chili flakes (optional)
3	tablespoons prepared capers, drained

1. Bring water for pasta to a boil over high heat. To the boiling water, add broccoli and co until broccoli turns bright green and is slightly tender when pierced, about 1 minute. Remove broccoli from boiling water with a slotted spoon and set aside until step 4.

2. Add carrots to boiling water. Cook until carrots are tender when pierced, about 6 minutes. Without removing carrots, add pasta and spinach leaves to boiling water. Coo until pasta is just tender, 2 to 3 minutes. Drain pasta and vegetables well; keep warm.

3. Meanwhile, in nonstick skillet, lightly brown zucchini, mushrooms, green onions, and garlic. Add broth, tomatoes, and chili flakes. Bring mixture to a boil over high heat; reduce heat to keep warm.

4. In large serving bowl, combine pasta-vegetable mixture and sautéed vegetable-broth mixture, broccoli, and capers. Transfer to a serving bowl or individual plates. Serve.

PASTA TOSSED WITH SEASONED OLIVE OIL AND FRESH BASIL

Serves 6
Prep. time: 15 minutes
Cooking time: 20 minutes

MENU PLANNING TIPS

The seasoned oil adds the flavor to this pasta toss. Experiment with different seasonings for your oil to change the flavor of this dish totally.

³/₄	pound dried linguine *or* fettuccine
1	onion, chopped
2	tablespoons hot chili olive oil *or* olive oil and ¹/₂ teaspoon hot chili flakes *(note: use any herb- or garlic-seasoned olive oil you prefer)*
2-4	cloves garlic, minced (depending on preference)
2	pounds ripe tomatoes, rinsed, cored, and coarsely chopped
2	cups firmly packed fresh basil leaves, slivered
	or
2	cups firmly packed fresh spinach leaves, slivered, and 1-2 tablespoons dried basil
	salt to taste optional
	Parmesan cheese *or* Cheeseless "Parmesan" Cheese *(p. 127)* (optional)

1. Bring water for pasta to a boil over high heat. Add pasta; cook until tender, 8 to 10 minutes. Drain well; pour into a wide serving bowl.

2. In a 10- to 12-inch frying pan over medium-high heat, combine onion and oil; stir often until onion is golden, about 8 to 10 minutes. Add garlic and cook an additional 2 minute

3. Add tomatoes. (If less-juicy sauce is desired, cut tomatoes in half crosswise and squee out and discard seeds before chopping.) Turn heat to high and stir until tomatoes are hot, 2 to 3 minutes. Remove from heat, stir in slivered basil and salt, and pour over pasta. Sprinkle with fresh grated Parmesan to taste, if desired.

FETTUCCINE PRIMAVERA "ALFREDO"

16	ounces fettuccine pasta
1-2	tablespoons olive oil
	salt (optional)
1/2-1	onion, chopped small
1	red pepper, chopped
4	garlic cloves, minced
4	carrots, thinly sliced
2	small zucchini, sliced
3	cups broccoli, cut in bite-size pieces
	Parmesan cheese *or* Cheeseless "Parmesan" Cheese *(p. 127)* (optional)

"ALFREDO" SAUCE:

10	ounces tofu, soft
2	tablespoons olive oil
1½	tablespoons lemon juice
1	tablespoon honey
½	teaspoon salt
¼	cup tofu *or* soy *or* nonfat milk
¼	teaspoon garlic, granulated
¼	teaspoon onion powder
¼	teaspoon McKay's Chicken-Style Seasoning *or* Chicken-like Seasoning *(p. 121)* (optional)

1. In large pan, bring water to boil for pasta. Add pasta and cook until tender. Drain; toss pasta with 1 tablespoon olive oil and salt to taste (optional).

2. In nonstick skillet, add olive oil, onion, and red pepper; sauté until just tender. Add thinly sliced carrots, zucchini, and broccoli and cook until tender. Add garlic and sauté an additional 2 minutes.

3. In blender, combine all the "Alfredo" sauce ingredients and blend until smooth.

4. Toss the cooked vegetables into the warm pasta. Then add the "Alfredo" sauce and mix to coat pasta evenly with sauce. Serve immediately. Top with freshly grated Parmesan cheese, if desired.

Serves 6
Prep. time: 10 minutes
Cooking time: 10 minutes

MENU PLANNING TIPS

This delicious cholesterol-free fettuccine can be enjoyed even while trying to watch your weight or on a low-cholesterol diet. The sauce is made with tofu blended in. Don't let this stop you from trying this recipe! When the tofu is blended with other seasonings, it takes on the flavor of the seasonings and adds that thick, creamy consistency to the sauce. Try adding fresh herbs to the sauce for variety. Developing a healthy fettuccine Alfredo sauce was challenging, but this sauce won First Place with many. Add a fresh green salad, and you'll have another heart-healthy meal.

VEGETABLE LASAGNA

VEGETABLE LASAGNA

Serves 12-15
Prep. time: 20 minutes
Cooking time: 45 minutes

1   18-ounce box dried lasagna noodles

2   large carrots, sliced

2   cups broccoli florets in bite-size pieces

VEGETABLE TOMATO SAUCE:

1   tablespoon olive oil

2   stalks celery, sliced

1   large sweet red bell pepper, chopped

2   small zucchini, sliced

2   small yellow squash, sliced

4   green onions, sliced *or* chopped

4-6 garlic cloves, minced

4   tablespoons fresh basil leaves *or* 4 teaspoons dried basil

2   tablespoons fresh oregano *or* 2 teaspoons dried oregano

½   teaspoon salt (optional)

8   cups diced tomatoes

1   6-ounce can tomato paste

4   tablespoons lemon juice

4   tablespoons sugar *or* honey

HERBED TOFU CHEESE MIXTURE:

Dairy option: *(substitute ricotta cheese and 2 egg whites, slightly beaten, for tofu)*

1   pound tofu (2 cups), blended or mashed

2   tablespoons olive oil

1   tablespoon fresh lemon juice

1   tablespoon honey

2   teaspoons garlic powder

1   teaspoon dried basil

1. Bring water for lasagna noodles to a boil over high heat, and add pasta to boiling water. Cook until pasta is just tender, 8 to 10 minutes. Drain noodles and lay out flat to cool until ready to assemble lasagna.

2. In separate saucepan or covered casserole dish for microwaving, steam the carrots and broccoli until tender. Let cool until ready to assemble.

3. In nonstick skillet, add olive oil and heat. Add celery, red peppers, zucchini, and yellow squash; cook until tender. Add green onions, garlic, basil, oregano, and salt (optional). Continue to cook for 2 minutes. Add tomatoes, tomato paste, lemon juice, and sugar or honey. Add the steamed carrots and broccoli.

4. In blender, combine tofu *(or ricotta cheese and egg whites)*, olive oil, lemon juice, honey, garlic powder, and dried basil; blend until smooth.

5. To assemble: In 9" x 13" lasagna pan with 3-inch sides, sprayed with nonstick vegetable spray, add 3 cups of the vegetable tomato sauce. Top with a layer of lasagna noodles, slightly overlapping each piece. Top noodles with 3 cups of vegetable sauce mixture. Spoon onto the sauce half of the cheese mixture in three strips down the noodles. Repeat with second layer of noodles, the remaining vegetable tomato sauce (approximately 3 cups), and the remaining cheese mixture. Bake immediately, or refrigerate or freeze for baking later. Bake for 45 minutes at 350°F, or until top is lightly browned and casserole is bubbly. Drizzle small amount of reserved vegetable tomato sauce over individual portions just before serving.

MENU PLANNING TIPS

This lasagna is a real winner with everyone! Because this dish can be made ahead and frozen or refrigerated until later, it works great for entertaining. Although I make this recipe with both the dairy option and the tofu option, most people prefer the herbed tofu cheese mixture. The homemade vegetable tomato sauce is the key to the rich flavor, without the cheese or meat. Reserve a small amount of vegetable tomato sauce and drizzle across the top of each serving of lasagna.

RICE AND COUSCOUS

Brown Rice With Vegetables
and Tomato Pesto

Pesto Rice and Beans

Stir-fried Asian Vegetables

Spring Vegetable Curry

Teriyaki Stir-fry Over Rice

Grilled Vegetables Over Rice

Hearty Rice Skillet

Herbed "Chicken" Couscous
and Vegetables

Garden Vegetable Couscous

Couscous Alfresco

Curried "Chicken"
and Broccoli Couscous

Basil-roasted Vegetables
Over Couscous

Roasted-Pepper Bruschetta

Pesto Risotto

Basmati Rice Seasoned With
Dried Fruits and Nuts

Vegetable Medley Quiche
in Rice Crust

BROWN RICE WITH VEGETABLES AND TOMATO PESTO

Serves 10
Prep. time: 15 minutes
Cooking time: 30 minutes

1	tablespoon oil
1	medium onion, chopped
4	cloves garlic, minced
1½	cups uncooked brown rice
3	cups water
3	teaspoons McKay's Chicken-Style Seasoning *or* Chicken-like Seasoning *(p. 121)*
4	small carrots, sliced
1	cup green beans, cut in 1-inch lengths
2	cups broccoli florets
2	small zucchini *or* yellow summer squash, sliced
½	cup tomato pesto (recipe below)

1. Heat 1 tablespoon oil in 2-quart saucepan over medium-high heat. Add onion and garlic; cook and stir 3 minutes. Add rice; cook and stir 2 minutes. Gradually add water and McKay's Chicken-Style Seasoning or Chicken-like Seasoning. Bring to a boil over medium-high heat. Reduce heat to low; simmer, covered, 30 to 40 minutes, or until rice is tender and liquid is absorbed.

2. Heat 3 tablespoons water or olive oil in large, nonstick skillet over medium heat. Add carrots and beans; cook and stir 4 minutes. Add squash and broccoli; cook and stir 5 to 7 minutes until vegetables are crisp-tender. Combine rice mixture and vegetable mixture in large bowl. Gently toss with ½ cup tomato pesto.

TOMATO PESTO:

Makes 1¼ cups

1	lemon
1	8-ounce jar sun-dried tomatoes packed in oil, undrained
1	large roasted red pepper (optional)
2	cloves garlic, minced
5	teaspoons fresh oregano, chopped, *or* 1½ teaspoons dried oregano
½	teaspoon sugar *or* honey
	salt to taste (if not using the cheese)
2	tablespoons freshly grated Parmesan cheese *or* Cheeseless "Parmesan" Cheese *(p. 127)* (optional)

1. Wash lemon; finely grate colored portion of lemon peel. Measure 2 teaspoons lemon peel and set aside.

2. Place lemon peel, sun-dried tomatoes, roasted red pepper, garlic, oregano, and sweetener of choice in food processor. Process until almost smooth, scraping side of bowl occasionally. Add salt or Parmesan cheese and stir until well combined. (Remaining pesto can be covered and refrigerated up to one week.)

PESTO RICE AND BEANS

Serves 8
Prep. time: 10 minutes
Cooking time: 30 minutes

¼   cup walnuts

½   pound fresh green beans

1   large clove garlic

1   cup packed fresh basil leaves, rinsed

¼   cup olive oil

3½   cups water

3½   teaspoons McKay's Chicken-Style Seasoning *or* Chicken-like Seasoning *(p. 121)*

2   cups cannellini (white kidney) beans

1   cup uncooked long-grain brown rice

½   teaspoon salt (optional)

1.   Preheat oven to 350°F. Spread walnuts in single layer on small, nonstick baking sheet. Bake 8 to 10 minutes until golden brown, stirring frequently.

2.   Place green beans in colander; rinse well under cold running water. To prepare beans, snap off stem end from each bean, pulling off strings, if present. (Young, tender beans may not have strings.)

3.   Cut green beans into 1-inch pieces; set aside.

4.   To prepare basil pesto: Place garlic, basil, oil, and walnuts in food processor. Cover; process using on/off pulsing action until coarsely ground.

5.   In saucepan, combine water and McKay's Chicken-Style Seasoning or Chicken-like Seasoning. Then add canned cannellini beans, with liquid, and heat thoroughly. Stir in rice; simmer, covered, for 10 minutes. Add green beans; simmer, covered, another 15 minutes, or until rice is tender.

6.   Stir in basil pesto. Transfer to large serving bowl. Garnish with plum tomatoes and Italian parsley, if desired.

STIR-FRIED ASIAN VEGETABLES

Serves 6
Prep. time: 10 minutes
Cooking time: 8 minutes

MENU PLANNING TIPS

This Asian stir-fry can be served as a side dish or spooned over rice or couscous for a complete meal. Try adding tofu or any meat substitute of choice, and exchange the vegetables for ones you have on hand for variety. Remember, the stir-frying doesn't have to be limited to Chinese dishes. Use stir-fried vegetables with pasta primavera or fajitas.

¾   cup water

1   teaspoon McKay's Chicken-Style Seasoning *or* Chicken-like Seasoning *(p. 121)*

1   tablespoon cornstarch

2   tablespoons low-sodium soy sauce

½   teaspoon sugar *or* honey

1   tablespoon canola oil *or* water

1   cup carrots, diagonally sliced

1   cup celery, diagonally sliced

½   cup onions, chopped

1½   cups snow peas, trimmed

1   15-ounce can whole baby corn, drained

½   cup mushrooms, halved

1.   Combine first five ingredients in a small bowl; stir with a wire whisk until well blended. Set aside.

2.   Heat oil or water in a wok or large nonstick skillet over high heat. Add carrots, celery, and onions; stir-fry 2 minutes. Add snow peas, corn, and mushrooms; stir-fry 2 more minutes. Add broth mixture; stir-fry 1 minute, or until thick and bubbly.

SPRING VEGETABLE CURRY

Serves 6-8
Prep. time: 15 minutes
Cooking time: 35-45 minutes

1	recipe curry powder (below)
1	cup uncooked dried split green peas
2	medium carrots
1	medium zucchini
2½	cups water
2½	teaspoons McKay's Chicken-Style Seasoning *or* Chicken-like Seasoning *(p. 121)*
	salt to taste
1	tablespoon olive oil
2	cups onions, chopped
4	cloves garlic, minced
2	cups frozen cauliflowerets
1½	cups unsweetened coconut *or* tofu *or* soy *or* nonfat evaporated milk
¼	teaspoon crushed red pepper
½	cup fresh *or* frozen green peas
1½	cups tomatoes, seeded and chopped
6-8	cups hot cooked brown rice

CURRY POWDER:

Combine following ingredients in small bowl and mix well:

2	teaspoons ground cumin
1	teaspoon ground ginger
1	teaspoon turmeric
½	teaspoon ground cinnamon
¼	teaspoon ground mace
¼	teaspoon ground cardamom
¼	teaspoon dry mustard

1. Prepare Curry Powder; set aside.
2. Rinse split peas thoroughly in colander under cold running water, picking out debris and any blemished peas; set aside.
3. Wash and peel carrots; cut into ¼-inch diagonal slices. Set aside.
4. Cut tip and stem from zucchini; slice in half lengthwise, then cut diagonal slices ¼-inch thick. Set aside.
5. Combine water, McKay's Chicken-Style Seasoning or Chicken-like Seasoning and 1 tablespoon Curry Powder in medium saucepan. Bring to a boil over high heat. Stir in split peas. Reduce heat to low; simmer, covered, 15 minutes.
6. Heat oil in large skillet over medium-high heat. Add onions; cook and stir 3 minutes, or until tender. Add carrots and garlic; cook and stir 5 to 7 minutes until carrots are crisp-tender. Add to seasoned, partially cooked split peas in saucepan.
7. Stir in cauliflowerets, milk of choice, zucchini, crushed red pepper, and salt to taste; simmer, covered, 20 to 25 minutes, until split peas are tender.
8. Stir in green peas and tomatoes just before serving.
9. Serve Spring Vegetable Curry over hot rice.

MENU PLANNING TIPS

This spicy one-dish meal is for all the curry lovers out there.

TERIYAKI STIR-FRY OVER RICE

Serves 6-8
Prep. time: 10 minutes
Cooking time: 20 minutes

2   large potatoes, chopped

2   carrots, sliced

1   tablespoon olive oil

1   small onion, chopped

½   red bell pepper, chopped

2   celery stalks, sliced

4   garlic cloves, minced

½   cup roasted peanuts *or* nuts of choice

4-6   cups cooked, long-grain brown rice

TERIYAKI SAUCE:

½   cup low-sodium soy sauce

¼   cup brown sugar *or* honey

½   tablespoon cornstarch

2   tablespoons water

1. Steam potatoes and carrots until tender. Set aside and keep warm.

2. Stir-fry over medium-high heat in a nonstick skillet in olive oil the onion, red pepper, and celery until tender, about 6 minutes. Add garlic and cook an additional 2 minutes. Add steamed potatoes and carrots and toss well. Toss in ½ cup peanuts or nuts of choice, and serve on a bed of rice.

3. To prepare Teriyaki Sauce: In small bowl combine ½ tablespoon cornstarch with 2 tablespoons water and stir until cornstarch is dissolved. Cook until sauce comes to a boil and is slightly thickened. Add more water if a thinner consistency is desired. Add soy sauce and sweetener of choice.

SUCCESSFUL STIR-FRY TIPS

1. Prepare the ingredients before heating the wok, and have them close at hand. Cut vegetables and any vegetarian meat or tofu into small, similar sizes. You can marinate the meat substitute, if desired.

2. Add the oil or water when the wok is hot. Swirl the oil or water around the bottom and sides of wok to thoroughly heat oil or water.

3. Stir-fry aromatics, such as ginger and garlic, until just fragrant. You can remove them after they've flavored the oil, or leave them in the wok.

4. Add any vegetarian meat or tofu and let it sit for a few seconds to brown before stirring. Don't crowd the pan. Cook ingredients until just done, then transfer them to a different bowl.

5. Cook the vegetables until crisp-tender. For dense vegetables, add a bit of liquid to the wok; cover, and steam.

6. Return the vegetarian meat or tofu to the wok and add a sauce that has a thickener in it, such as cornstarch *(see Stir-fried Asian Vegetables recipe, p. 74)*. Quickly toss the meat and vegetables with the sauce to cover evenly. Serve immediately.

MENU PLANNING TIPS

This recipe is easy to prepare, and the flavor combination is delicious. Serve it over a bed of hot rice, and top it with Teriyaki Sauce (below).

GRILLED VEGETABLES OVER RICE

Serves 6-8
Prep. time: 10 minutes
Cooking time: 10 minutes

1	green bell pepper, cut in wedges
2	carrots, thinly sliced
1	cup yellow summer squash, sliced
1	small onion, cut into wedges
2	garlic cloves, thinly sliced
1½	teaspoons olive oil
1½	teaspoons fresh oregano, chopped, *or* ½ teaspoon dried oregano
1½	teaspoons fresh basil, chopped, *or* ½ teaspoon dried basil
¼	teaspoon salt (optional)
1	large tomato, cut into eight wedges
1	cup cannellini (white kidney) beans *or* garbanzos
4	cups cooked brown rice

1. Prepare and cut vegetables. The vegetables should be approximately the same size so that they are done at the same time. The carrots should be very thin so they will be cooked enough in 10 minutes. Combine in mixing bowl all ingredients, except the tomatoes, rice, and beans. Toss vegetable mixture lightly to glaze the vegetables with olive oil, herbs, and salt.

2. Spoon vegetable mixture onto a broiler pan or cookie sheet coated with nonstick cooking spray. Broil 5 minutes; stir tomatoes and beans into vegetable mixture. Baste with additional marinade and broil for 5 additional minutes, or until vegetables are tender and lightly browned. Tomatoes and beans should be just warmed. If you prefer the tomatoes softer, add at the beginning of the 10 minutes.

3. Serve roasted vegetables over a bed of rice.

HEARTY RICE SKILLET

1	15-ounce can black beans *or* kidney beans, rinsed and drained
1	14$\frac{1}{2}$-ounce can crushed *or* diced tomatoes
1	cup frozen corn
$\frac{1}{2}$	cup frozen peas
$\frac{1}{2}$	cup frozen lima beans
$\frac{1}{2}$	cup frozen green beans, 1-inch pieces
1	cup water
$\frac{3}{4}$	cup quick-cooking brown rice
$\frac{1}{2}$	teaspoon dried thyme *or* dillweed, crushed
	dash of bottled hot pepper sauce *or* salsa (optional)
1	8-ounce can tomato purée
1	tablespoon lemon juice
1	tablespoon sugar *or* honey
$\frac{1}{3}$	cup slivered almonds

1. Combine beans, crushed tomatoes, corn, peas, lima beans, green beans, water, uncooked rice, and thyme in a large skillet. Stir in hot pepper sauce or hot salsa, if desired. Bring to boiling; reduce heat. Simmer, covered, for 12 to 14 minutes or until rice is tender. Stir in puréed tomatoes, lemon juice, and sugar or honey; heat through.

2. Spread the almonds in a thin layer in a shallow baking pan. Bake in a 250°F oven, stirring once or twice, for 5 minutes, or until the almonds are golden.

3. To serve, stir in toasted almonds. Sprinkle with shredded mozzarella or tofu cheese.

Serves 4
Prep. time: 10 minutes
Cooking time: 15 minutes

HERBED "CHICKEN" COUSCOUS AND VEGETABLES

1	cup fresh mushrooms, sliced
1	12$\frac{1}{2}$-ounce can Worthington Low-Fat FriChik, chopped
	or
1	10-ounce package firm tofu, cubed
1	teaspoon olive *or* canola oil
1	cup green peas, frozen
1	tablespoon fresh parsley, chopped
$\frac{1}{2}$	teaspoon dried basil, crushed
$\frac{1}{8}$	teaspoon dried oregano, crushed
$\frac{1}{4}$	teaspoon salt (optional)
$\frac{1}{4}$	teaspoon garlic powder
$\frac{2}{3}$	cup uncooked couscous
1	medium tomato, peeled, seeded, and chopped

1. In nonstick skillet over medium-high heat, cook mushrooms and Worthington Low-Fat FriChik or tofu cubes in oil of choice until tender and lightly browned.

2. Stir in peas, parsley, basil, oregano, salt, and garlic powder, and add 1 cup water to saucepan; bring to boil. Remove from heat; stir in couscous. Cover and let stand for 5 minutes. Stir in tomatoes. Serve immediately.

Serves 4
Prep. time: 10 minutes
Cooking time: 10 minutes

MENU PLANNING TIPS
Couscous, a North African staple, is a light dish of tiny pasta made from semolina, a coarsely ground durum wheat. Serve it as you would rice or grains. In this recipe I add seasonings, mushrooms, and a chicken substitute. You can add an additional cooked vegetable on the side, a tossed green salad, and whole-grain bread to complete this meal.

GARDEN VEGETABLE COUSCOUS

Serves 8-10
Prep. time: 10 minutes
Cooking time: 15 minutes

MENU PLANNING TIPS

This pasta tastes wonderful with the garden vegetable topping and the beans and peanuts. These ingredients combine to give you a great one-dish meal. Serve with whole-grain bread and enjoy.

1	large onion, cut into thin wedges
2	cloves garlic, minced
1	teaspoon canola *or* olive oil
2	cups carrots, thinly sliced
1	teaspoon dried basil, crushed
¹⁄₂-1	teaspoon ground cumin, to taste
¹⁄₄	teaspoon salt
2	medium zucchini, quartered lengthwise and cut into ¹⁄₂-inch pieces (2¹⁄₂ cups)
1	15-ounce can garbanzo beans, rinsed and drained
1	14¹⁄₂-ounce can whole tomatoes, crushed
2	teaspoons cornstarch
2	cups water
2	teaspoons McKay's Chicken-Style Seasoning *or* Chicken-like Seasoning *(p. 121)*
1	cup uncooked couscous
¹⁄₄	cup unsalted dry roasted peanuts, chopped in large pieces

1. Cook onion and garlic in hot oil in a large saucepan over medium-low heat till crisp-tender. Stir in carrots, ¹⁄₂ cup water, basil, cumin, and salt; bring to boil. Reduce heat, cover, and simmer for 10 minutes.

2. Stir in zucchini, garbanzo beans, and tomatoes. Cover and cook for 2 minutes. Stir together 2 tablespoons water and cornstarch. Stir into tomato mixture. Cook and stir until thickened and bubbly. Cook and stir 2 minutes more.

3. In separate saucepan, add 2 teaspoons McKay's Chicken-Style Seasoning or Chicken-like Seasoning to 2 cups water, and bring to a boil. Add couscous; cover and let stand 5 minutes, or until liquid is absorbed; fluff with fork. Serve vegetable mixture over hot couscous. Sprinkle with peanuts before serving.

COUSCOUS ALFRESCO

Serves 4
Prep. time: 10 minutes
Cooking time: 15 minutes

2	tablespoons pine nuts *or* chopped walnuts
1	teaspoon olive oil
2	cloves garlic, minced
2	cups water
2	teaspoons McKay's Chicken-Style Seasoning *or* Chicken-like Seasoning *(p. 121)*
¹⁄₄	teaspoon dried basil
¹⁄₄	teaspoon dried oregano
2	cups uncooked whole-wheat couscous
10	fresh asparagus spears, trimmed and cut into 1-inch pieces
2	medium tomatoes, seeded and diced
¹⁄₄	cup ripe olives, sliced

1. In medium-size saucepan over medium heat, add pine nuts; shake pan frequently until nuts are lightly browned. Remove from saucepan; set aside.

2. Heat olive oil in same saucepan over medium heat. Add garlic; sauté 2 minutes. Add water, McKay's Chicken-Style Seasoning or Chicken-like Seasoning, basil, and oregano. Bring to a boil. Stir in asparagus. Reduce heat; cover, and simmer 1 minute. Stir in couscous; cover and remove from heat. Let stand 5 minutes.

3. Fluff couscous lightly with a fork. Stir in nuts, tomatoes, and olives. Serve immediately.

CURRIED "CHICKEN" AND BROCCOLI COUSCOUS

1	12½-ounce can Worthington FriChik, cut in thin strips
	or
1	10-ounce package firm tofu, cut in 1-inch cubes
2	teaspoons curry powder, divided
2	teaspoons olive oil, divided
½	cup onion, chopped
2	cups water
2	teaspoons McKay's Chicken-Style Seasoning *or* Chicken-like Seasoning *(p. 121)*
1½	cups broccoli florets
½	cup red bell pepper, chopped
½	cup raisins (optional)
2	teaspoons firmly packed brown sugar *or* honey *and/or* molasses
1	cup uncooked whole-wheat couscous

1. Sprinkle one side of FriChik strips or tofu cubes with 1 teaspoon curry powder.

2. Heat 1 teaspoon olive oil in a large skillet over medium-high heat. Add FriChik or tofu; sauté 2 minutes on each side, or until lightly browned. Remove from skillet, and keep warm.

3. Heat remaining olive oil in same skillet. Add onion; sauté 2 minutes, stirring frequently. Add water and McKay's Chicken-Style Seasoning or Chicken-like Seasoning, broccoli, red bell pepper, raisins, brown sugar or honey, remaining 1 teaspoon curry powder, and reserved FriChik or tofu to cooked onions. Bring to a boil. Stir in couscous, cover. Remove from heat; let stand 5 minutes. Toss couscous lightly with a fork before serving.

Serves 4
Prep. time: 10 minutes
Cooking time: 15 minutes

MENU PLANNING TIPS

This meal is so quick to make—your dinner is ready in 15 minutes. This dish includes your grains and vegetables all together to make a complete meal.

BASIL-ROASTED VEGETABLES OVER COUSCOUS

Serves 4
Prep. time: 10 minutes
Cooking time: 35 minutes

1/4 cup fresh basil, minced

2 tablespoons lemon juice

1 tablespoon olive oil

1/4 teaspoon salt

2 garlic cloves, minced

2 medium zucchini, cut into 1-inch slices

1 medium red bell pepper, cut into 1-inch pieces

1 medium yellow bell pepper, cut into 1-inch pieces

1 medium red onion, cut into eight wedges

1 cup mushrooms, halved

3 cups hot, cooked whole-wheat couscous

1. Preheat oven to 425°F.

2. Combine first five ingredients in a large bowl; stir well. Add zucchini, bell peppers, onion, and mushrooms; toss well to coat. Arrange vegetables in a single layer on a shallow roasting pan. Bake at 425°F for 25 to 30 minutes, or until tender and browned, stirring occasionally.

3. Spoon roasted vegetables over couscous. Garnish with fresh basil sprigs and feta cheese, if desired.

ROASTED-PEPPER BRUSCHETTA

Serves 10
Prep. time: 30 minutes
Cooking time: 30 minutes

2 medium-size sweet red peppers

2 medium-size sweet yellow peppers

1 medium-size sweet green pepper

3 garlic cloves, unpeeled

1 medium-size loaf round Italian bread

1 tablespoon olive oil

1 tablespoon lemon juice

fresh Parmesan cheese, grated, *or* Cheeseless "Parmesan" Cheese *(p. 127)* (optional)

1. Heat oven to 450°F. Place whole peppers and garlic on rimmed baking sheet. Bake peppers and garlic 30 minutes, turning peppers every 10 minutes. Remove vegetables from oven. Set aside garlic and carefully place hot peppers in brown paper bag; close bag tightly, allowing peppers to steam and cool until easy to handle—about 20 minutes.

2. Meanwhile, reduce oven temperature to 350°F. Cut bread into 11 slices, each about 1/2-inch thick. Place the two end slices on ungreased baking sheet. Cut the remaining nine slices in half and place on baking sheet. Toast bread 10 minutes, or until lightly browned.

3. When peppers are cool, peel, halve, and seed them and chop them into 1/4-inch cubes. Peel garlic cloves. In medium-size bowl, crush garlic with back of wooden spoon. Add roasted sweet peppers, oil, and lemon juice; toss to combine. Add salt to taste, if desired.

4. Divide pepper mixture on toasted bread. Garnish with freshly grated Parmesan cheese, if desired. Serve warm or at room temperature.

MENU PLANNING TIPS

Relish the robust flavor of Italy in this colorful appetizer, made from a pungent mixture of roasted peppers and roasted garlic. Serve over toasted Italian bread with the Pesto Risotto *(p. 84)* for an elegant light meal the next time you entertain. To shorten preparation time, use canned roasted red peppers, drained.

PESTO RISOTTO

Serves 6
Prep. time: 10 minutes
Cooking time: 25 minutes

MENU PLANNING TIPS

The Italian dish of Pesto Risotto is made with arborio rice, because it is creamy on the outside and slightly firm in the center, which is more characteristic of risotto. Serve this with Roasted-Pepper Bruschetta *(p. 83)* and tossed green salad for a light Italian dinner.

	pesto (recipe below)
$4^1/_2$	cups water
4	teaspoons McKay's Chicken-Style Seasoning *or* Chicken-like Seasoning *(p. 121)*
2	tablespoons lemon juice
2	teaspoons olive oil
$1^1/_2$	cups arborio rice, uncooked
2	cloves garlic, minced
	salt to taste (optional)
	fresh basil sprigs

1. Prepare pesto, set aside.

2. In 2-quart saucepan, heat water, McKay's Chicken-Style Seasoning or Chicken-like Seasoning, and lemon juice to boiling. Remove from heat.

3. In large skillet, heat oil over medium heat. Add rice and garlic; stir constantly for 3 minutes, or until rice starts to brown.

4. Add $^1/_2$ cup of the hot broth mixture to the sautéed rice and garlic; cook, stirring constantly, until all the liquid has been absorbed. Continue to cook, stirring constantly and adding broth mixture $^1/_2$ cup at a time until all liquid has been absorbed and rice is creamy but slightly al dente—about 20 to 25 minutes. If desired, add salt to taste. Pour risotto into serving dish.

5. Spoon pesto onto risotto in a spiral pattern; top with basil sprigs and serve immediately. (This will become sticky if allowed to stand before serving.)

PESTO:

$^1/_2$	cup packed fresh basil leaves, chopped
$^1/_4$	cup fresh parsley sprigs, chopped
2	tablespoons pine nuts or chopped walnuts (Try toasting walnuts for a different taste.)
1	clove garlic, minced
$^1/_4$	cup olive oil

1. Place first four ingredients in the blender and process until basil, parsley, and pine nuts are chopped fine and form a paste. While machine is running, slowly pour in olive oil and process until well blended. Add freshly grated Parmesan cheese, if desired. Spoon pesto onto risotto, following previous recipe.

BASMATI RICE SEASONED WITH DRIED FRUITS AND NUTS

Serves 6
Prep. time: 10 minutes
Cooking time: 20-30 minutes

1-2	tablespoons olive *or* canola oil
1	small onion, minced
$^{1}/_{2}$	cup basmati rice
$3^{1}/_{4}$	cups water
$^{3}/_{4}$	teaspoon salt
$^{1}/_{4}$	teaspoon ground cinnamon
$^{1}/_{4}$	teaspoon ground allspice
$^{1}/_{4}$	cup raisins
$^{1}/_{4}$	cup dried cranberries
$^{1}/_{2}$	cup dried apricot halves, coarsely chopped
$^{1}/_{2}$	cup pecans, toasted and coarsely chopped

1. Sauté in saucepan over medium heat, olive oil and onion, stirring, until soft, about 10 minutes.

2. Meanwhile, rinse the rice well and drain. When the onion is ready, add the rice, water, salt, cinnamon, allspice, raisins, cranberries, and apricots to the saucepan. Bring to a boil; reduce the heat to low, cover, and cook without stirring for 20 minutes. Do not remove the cover. After 20 minutes, uncover and check to see if the rice is tender and the water is absorbed. If not, cover and cook for a few minutes longer until the rice is done.

3. Toasting the pecans brings out the full flavor and aroma of the nuts. Preheat oven to 250°F. Spread the nuts in a single layer on a baking sheet and toast in the oven until they just begin to change color, 5 to 10 minutes. Remove from oven.

4. Add the toasted pecans to the rice and toss to combine. Transfer to a warmed serving dish and serve immediately.

VEGETABLE MEDLEY QUICHE IN RICE CRUST

VEGETABLE MEDLEY QUICHE IN RICE CRUST

3	cups cooked short-grain rice
1	tablespoon olive oil
2	stalks celery, chopped
1	medium onion, chopped
1	red bell pepper, chopped
2	garlic cloves, minced
1	zucchini *or* yellow squash, halved lengthwise and sliced
3	cups broccoli, cut into bite-size pieces
1	teaspoon McKay's Chicken-Style Seasoning *or* Chicken-like Seasoning *(p. 121)*
1	teaspoon garlic powder
¼	teaspoon salt

TOFU FILLING:

2	cups tofu, soft
1	tablespoon lemon juice
1	tablespoon olive oil
1	tablespoon honey
2	teaspoons garlic powder
1	teaspoon dried basil
¼	teaspoon salt
2-4	tablespoons tofu milk *or* nonfat milk

Serves 6
Prep. time: 10 minutes
Cooking time: 35 minutes

1. Prepare rice as directed on package. Short-grain rice will be stickier and hold together to form crust. Spray nonstick cooking spray into 9-inch pie plate. Press rice into pie plate to form a crust that is approximately ½-inch thick.

2. In nonstick skillet over medium-high heat, heat olive oil, celery, onion, and red bell pepper until tender. Add garlic and cook an additional 2 minutes. Add zucchini, broccoli, McKay's Chicken-Style Seasoning or Chicken-like Seasoning, garlic powder, and salt. Cook until vegetables are tender.

3. In blender, combine tofu filling ingredients. Blend until smooth. Add more milk of choice for pourable consistency.

4. Combine cooked vegetables and tofu mixture and mix well. Pour into rice pie shell. Bake at 375°F for 30 to 35 minutes, or until knife inserted comes out clean and filling is light brown. Serve warm.

Main Dish Dinner

POTATOES

Garden-fresh Potato Toss

Roots at 500ºF

Garlic Potatoes With "Chicken"

Vegetable Potato Salad

Cheesy Potato Skins

Mexican Baked Potatoes With
Bean-and-Corn Salsa

GARDEN-FRESH POTATO TOSS

8	medium-size new potatoes, red *or* white, halved *or* quartered
1	teaspoon olive oil
1	large onion, chopped
1	red *or* green bell pepper, chopped
3	garlic cloves, minced
2	zucchini, sliced
1	yellow summer squash, sliced
1	tablespoon fresh thyme *or* ½ teaspoon dried thyme
¼	teaspoon salt (optional)
	fresh thyme sprigs for garnish

1. Microwave diced potatoes in small amount of water in covered casserole dish. Cook until tender, about 12 to 15 minutes. Drain water.

2. In nonstick skillet over medium-high heat, add olive oil, onion, and pepper, and cook until tender. Add garlic, and cook additional 1 to 2 minutes. Add zucchini and yellow summer squash and cook until tender.

3. To the cooked vegetables, add the chopped cooked potatoes, thyme, and salt; mix well. Serve warm. Add additional garlic powder, if desired. (Sometimes I add McKay's Chicken-Style Seasoning or Chicken-like Seasoning for variety.) Garnish with thyme sprigs.

Serves 6
Prep. time: 10 minutes
Cooking time: 20 minutes

MENU PLANNING TIPS
This easy-to-prepare potato dish is a great one-dish meal. Add different fresh or dried herbs for a variety in flavor. Serve with a salad and whole-grain rolls for a full meal.

ROOTS AT 500°F

1	large russet potato
2	teaspoons olive oil
¾	cup baby carrots
1	red onion, coarsely chopped
1	yam
1	beet
2	tablespoons green onion, thinly sliced
	garlic powder to taste (optional)
	salt to taste (optional)
	parsley sprigs for garnish

1. Scrub potato and cut into ¾-inch cubes.

2. In 500°F oven, heat oil in a 10"x15" roasting pan until hot, about 1½ minutes. Add cubed potato, carrots, and red onion. Cook 15 minutes, stirring after 10 minutes.

3. Meanwhile, peel yam and beet; cut each into about ½-inch cubes. Add to pan after potato has cooked 15 minutes; cook about 20 minutes more, stirring every 10 minutes, until potatoes are golden brown.

4. Spoon vegetables onto a platter; garnish with parsley. Add salt and garlic powder, if desired.

Serves 4
Prep. time: 10 minutes
Cooking time: 35 minutes

MENU PLANNING TIPS
Cooking at 500°F not only helps speed up the cooking process, but also enhances the flavor of the vegetables by caramelizing the natural sugars in the vegetables, which produces an even more naturally sweet flavor.

GARLIC POTATOES WITH "CHICKEN"

Serves 6
Prep. time: 10 minutes
Cooking time: 45 minutes

2	pounds thin-skinned red *and/or* white potatoes (about 18)
1	tablespoon olive oil
1	onion, quartered
1	12$\frac{1}{2}$-ounce can Worthington Low-Fat FriChik, cubed
	or
1	10-ounce package firm tofu, cubed
1	bulb garlic, cloves peeled
3	tablespoons dried tomatoes, rehydrated and minced
2	teaspoons fresh rosemary leaves
	salt to taste (optional)
	fresh rosemary sprigs for garnish

1. Scrub potatoes. In 500°F oven, heat oil in a 10"x15" roasting pan until hot, about 1$\frac{1}{2}$ minutes. Add potatoes and onion; shake pan to coat vegetables with oil. Cook 15 minutes, then add FriChik or tofu cubes and garlic and cook 30 minutes more, stirring vegetables every 10 minutes.

2. Stir tomatoes and rosemary leaves into potato mixture. Add salt to taste, if desired. Pour onto serving platter and garnish with rosemary sprigs.

VEGETABLE POTATO SALAD

Serves 4
Prep. time: 10 minutes
Cooking time: 15-20 minutes

1	cup water
$\frac{1}{2}$	teaspoon salt
$\frac{3}{4}$	pound whole tiny new potatoes, halved *or* quartered
1	pound asparagus, cut into 1-inch pieces (1$\frac{1}{3}$ cups)
1	medium carrot, cut into thin strips (1$\frac{1}{2}$ cups)
	Low-Fat Creamy Onion-Dill Dressing *(p. 122)* or Nondairy Creamy Onion-Dill Dressing *(p. 123)*
	fresh dill sprigs for garnish

1. Bring water and salt to boiling in a large saucepan. Add potatoes and cook, covered, for 8 minutes. Add asparagus and carrot; cook 4 to 8 minutes more, or until potatoes are tender and asparagus and carrot strips are crisp-tender. Drain well. Arrange vegetables in a shallow serving bowl; or chill, if desired, and serve as a cold salad.

2. Prepare Creamy Onion-Dill Dressing. Add enough milk to make it quite thin and pourable. The consistency of a French dressing is about right. If it is too thick, it will overpower the taste of the vegetables. Cover and chill until serving time.

3. Just before serving, spoon dressing over vegetables. You can spoon the dressing into the middle of the vegetables, or you can toss the dressing with the vegetables, covering them evenly. Garnish with fresh dill sprigs and serve.

CHEESY POTATO SKINS

4	russet baking potatoes
1	tablespoon olive oil
1/2	teaspoon granulated garlic
	salt to taste (optional)
1/2	cup tofu cheese, grated, *or* low-fat mozzarella cheese, grated
2	tablespoons green onions *or* chives, sliced *or* chopped
1/2	cup Nondairy Creamy Onion-Dill Dressing *(p. 123)* *or* Low-Fat Creamy Onion-Dill Dressing *(p. 122)*

1. Scrub potatoes and remove any bad spots. Slice in half lengthwise. If you use potatoes that are of uniform size, the potatoes will be done at the same time. Place cut potatoes on a baking sheet. Add olive oil and toss potatoes, covering lightly with oil. Then place with cut sides up and sprinkle with garlic granules and salt. Bake at 450°F for 10 minutes; check potatoes and rotate, if some areas are more done than others. Bake an additional 20 minutes, checking at 10 minutes. When potatoes are tender and lightly browned, remove from oven.

2. Add grated cheese of choice and green onions or chives and bake an additional 5 minutes. (Or add the bean-and-corn salsa, top with the cheese, and bake 5 minutes.)

3. Serve with Creamy Onion-Dill Dressing (or nonfat sour cream on the side for dipping).

Serves 8
Prep. time: 5 minutes
Cooking time: 30 minutes

MENU PLANNING TIPS

Try serving these baked potato skins with nonfat sour cream or Tofu Sour Cream *(p. 122)*, topped with chopped chives or green onions. For variety, top these skins with chili beans or bean-and-corn salsa *(p. 93)*. With these toppings this is very filling and can serve as your main course. The cheese-topped potato skins are a great appetizer or can be served with salad to make a light meal.

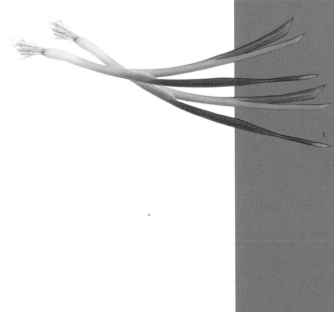

MEXICAN BAKED POTATOES WITH BEAN-AND-CORN SALSA

4	large baking potatoes
	bean-and-corn salsa (below)
$^1/_2$	cup grated tofu cheese *or* low-fat shredded mozzarella cheese
$^1/_2$	cup Tofu Sour Cream *(p. 122) or* low-fat sour cream (optional)

1. Bake potatoes until tender, approximately 35 minutes. To speed up preparation time, you can microwave the baking potatoes in a covered dish with a small amount of water for approximately 15 minutes, or until just tender.

2. Split the warm potatoes in half lengthwise. Top with the bean-and-corn salsa. Sprinkle with the grated cheese of choice. Bake for 5 minutes or microwave for 1 minute to melt the cheese. Serve immediately, and top with sour cream of choice, if desired.

BEAN-AND-CORN SALSA:

1	cup canned kidney *or* pinto beans, rinsed and drained
1	cup canned cannellini (white kidney) beans, rinsed and drained
$^3/_4$	cup canned corn, drained, *or* fresh corn, cut off cob
$^1/_4$	cup red bell pepper, chopped
$^1/_4$	cup fresh cilantro, chopped
$^1/_2$	cup fresh tomatoes, chopped
2-4	tablespoons canned green chilies, chopped
2	tablespoons red onion, minced (optional)
2-4	tablespoons scallions, chopped *or* minced
1	tablespoon lemon juice
$^1/_2$	teaspoon ground cumin
$^1/_8$	teaspoon chili powder (optional)
$^1/_4$	teaspoon garlic powder

In medium bowl, mix all ingredients. Cover and refrigerate for at least 1 hour. The flavor is enhanced when the salsa sits for at least an hour, but it can be served immediately. There will be leftover salsa to use for other meals, so cover and chill for later use.

Serves 4
Prep. time: 15 minutes
Cooking time:
15 *or* 35 minutes

MENU PLANNING TIPS
Try delicious bean-and-corn salsa over hot baked potato halves. You can serve low-fat sour cream or Nondairy Tofu Sour Cream as an additional topping. Use these same toppings to serve leftover baked potatoes—just warm the baked potatoes and add the salsa and sour cream of choice.

Main Dish Dinner

MEXICAN & LEGUMES
Bean Enchiladas

Vegetable Burritos Grande

Baked Enchilada Casserole

White Bean Quesadillas

Layered Bean Dip

Oven-baked Vegetable Fajitas

Tamale Pie

No-Guilt Refried Beans

Mazidra

Indian Lentils and Rice

BEAN ENCHILADAS

Serves 6
Prep. time: 15 minutes
Cooking time: 20 minutes

1	16-ounce can whole tomatoes, undrained
1	medium onion, chopped (1/2 cup)
2	cloves garlic, minced
1/4	cup fresh cilantro, chopped
1	teaspoon lemon juice
2	teaspoons honey
2-4	tablespoons canned green chilies (optional)
1	large tomato, seeded and diced
1	15-ounce can pinto beans, rinsed and drained
1	cup low-fat ricotta cheese *or* substitute the following:

TOFU CHEESE RECIPE, MIXED WELL:

1	cup firm tofu, well mashed
1	tablespoon olive oil
1	tablespoon lemon juice
1	teaspoon honey
1/2	teaspoon salt

1	cup zucchini, peeled and grated
1	small green pepper, chopped (1/2 cup)
1-2	teaspoons ground cumin
6	flour tortillas (8-10 inches in diameter)
1/2	cup tofu cheese *or* low-fat mozzarella *or* Monterey Jack, grated (optional)

1. Heat oven to 375°F. Spray rectangular baking dish, 11" x 7" x 1½", with nonstick cooking spray. Place tomatoes, onion, and garlic in blender or food processor. Cover and blend on high speed until smooth.

2. Cook blended mixture, 2 tablespoons cilantro, lemon juice, and honey in 2-quart saucepan over medium heat for 3 minutes, stirring occasionally. Add green chilies and fresh tomato and cook an additional 1 to 2 minutes. Remove from heat.

3. Mix beans, ricotta or tofu cheese mixture, grated zucchini, green pepper, cumin, and remaining cilantro.

4. Spread 1/2 cup of the cooked tomato mixture in baking dish. Spoon 1/2 cup of the bean mixture on one side of each tortilla. Roll up tortillas; place seam sides down on tomato mixture in baking dish. Spoon remaining tomato mixture over tortillas. Sprinkle with grated cheese. Bake 20 to 25 minutes, or until tomato mixture is bubbly and cheese is melted.

VEGETABLE BURRITOS GRANDE

Serves 8
Prep. time: 10 minutes
Cooking time: 10 minutes

1	tablespoon olive oil *or* water
1	medium carrot, scraped and shredded
1	small onion, chopped
1	garlic clove, minced
1	8-ounce can tomato purée
2	cups fresh broccoli florets
2	cups canned *or* frozen corn
1	15-ounce can black beans, drained and rinsed
1-2	teaspoons chili powder
1-2	teaspoons ground cumin
1/4	teaspoon salt
	dash of hot sauce (optional)
8	10-inch flour tortillas
1/2	cup tofu cheese *or* low-fat mozzarella cheese, grated (optional)

1. In large nonstick skillet with small amount of oil or water, cook carrots and onions over medium-high heat until tender. Add garlic and cook an additional 2 minutes. Stir in tomato purée, broccoli, corn, beans, chili powder, cumin, salt, and hot sauce. Cover and simmer 5 to 7 minutes.

2. Wrap flour tortillas in a paper towel and microwave on high for about 30 seconds to soften them. Keep them warm.

3. Spoon about 1/2 cup vegetable mixture evenly down center of each tortilla; sprinkle with cheese. Fold opposite sides of tortilla over filling, securing with a wooden toothpick, if necessary. Serve immediately with desired toppings of salsa *(p. 125)*, nonfat sour cream or Tofu Sour Cream *(p. 122),* and/or Guacamole *(p. 126)*.

BAKED ENCHILADA CASSEROLE

Serves 6-8
Prep. time: 10 minutes
Cooking time: 45 minutes

1	16-ounce can pinto beans, drained
1	16-ounce can chili beans, undrained
1	large onion, chopped
1/2-1	cup Thick and Chunky Salsa *(p. 125)* *or* Classic Fresh Salsa *(p. 125)* *or* purchased picante sauce
12	corn tortillas, cut into 1-inch squares
1-2	cups Cheeseless "Cheese" Sauce *(p. 127)* *or* low-fat cheddar cheese, grated
1	large tomato, chopped
2	cups head lettuce, chopped
	Guacamole *(p. 126)*
	nonfat sour cream *or* Tofu Sour Cream *(p. 122)*

1. In medium-size mixing bowl, combine beans, onion, and salsa; mix well.

2. Spray with nonstick cooking spray an 8" x 11" baking pan with 2" sides. Sprinkle 1 tablespoon water in bottom of pan. Layer pan with half of the corn tortilla pieces, half of the bean mix, and half of the cheese; repeat the layers.

3. Bake at 350°F for 45 minutes. Serve with chopped tomatoes, lettuce, guacamole, and sour cream of choice.

WHITE BEAN QUESADILLAS

2 cups canned cannellini (white kidney) beans *or* small white beans

1 cup roasted sweet red peppers, chopped

1 cup tofu cheese *or* low-fat Monterey Jack cheese, grated

½ teaspoon garlic powder

½ teaspoon dried basil

½ teaspoon dried oregano

8 large flour tortillas

1 teaspoon canola oil, divided, *or* nonstick vegetable spray

1. Warm beans and mash lightly.

2. Stir in the peppers, cheese, garlic powder, basil, and oregano.

3. Wrap the tortillas in a paper towel and microwave on high for about 30 seconds to soften them. Divide the bean mixture among the tortillas, spreading it to within 1 inch of the edges. Fold each tortilla in half.

4. In a medium nonstick skillet over medium heat, warm about ½ teaspoon of oil. Place quesadillas in the pan. Cook for 2 to 3 minutes, or until the bottoms are golden. Flip the quesadillas and gently press on them with a spatula to help the cheese melt. Cook for another 3 to 4 minutes. Remove from the pan

5. Continue, adding the remaining oil as needed until all the quesadillas are browned. You can eliminate the oil if you spray the skillet with nonstick cooking spray between each browning.

Serves 6-8
Prep. time: 10 minutes
Cooking time: 10 minutes

MENU PLANNING TIPS
These great-tasting quesadillas work as an appetizer or can be served with salsa, guacamole, and tossed green salad for a complete meal.

LAYERED BEAN DIP

1 30-ounce can pinto beans, blended smooth

½ teaspoon ground cumin

¼ teaspoon chili powder

¼ teaspoon granulated garlic

¼ teaspoon onion powder

1 4-ounce can green chilies, chopped

1-2 cups Cheeseless "Cheese" Sauce *(p. 127)*

chopped tomatoes *or* salsa for garnish

1. Blend beans, cumin, chili powder, garlic, and onion powder until smooth.

2. In 9-inch pie plate sprayed with nonstick cooking spray, spread an even layer of blended bean mixture. Sprinkle with chopped green chilies. Pour the uncooked Cheeseless "Cheese" Sauce over bean mixture about ¼ to ½ inch in thickness.

Serves 6
Prep. time: 5 minutes
Cooking time: 20-30 minutes

MENU PLANNING TIPS
Serve this bean dip with tortilla chips as an appetizer with any of the Mexican dishes in this section, or serve with salad as a light meal. You can also use the No-Guilt Refried Bean recipe *(p. 100)* to replace the first five ingredients. Garnish with chopped tomatoes or salsa of choice.

OVEN-BAKED VEGETABLE FAJITAS

Serves 4
Prep. time: 15 minutes
Cooking time: 15 minutes

1	medium red bell pepper, cut into 1-inch pieces
1	medium green bell pepper, cut into 1-inch pieces
2	zucchini *or* yellow squash, cut into 1-inch slices
1	large onion, cut into wedges
2	garlic cloves, thinly sliced
1	teaspoon olive oil
2	teaspoons fresh oregano, chopped, *or* ¾ teaspoon dried oregano
¼	teaspoon salt (optional)
1	large tomato, cut into eight wedges
2	cups cooked brown rice
2	cups canned chili beans
4	10-inch flour tortillas

1. Prepare and cut vegetables.

2. In mixing bowl combine peppers, squash, onion, garlic, olive oil, oregano, and salt. Toss vegetable mixture lightly to glaze the vegetables with oil and herbs.

3. Place vegetables onto a broiler pan or cookie sheet coated with nonstick cooking spray. Broil 5 minutes; add tomato wedges and stir into vegetable mixture, coating with marinade. Broil for 5 additional minutes, or until vegetables are just tender and lightly browned.

4. Assembly: Place ½ cup beans and ½ cup rice in flour tortillas. Top with grilled vegetables. Roll up tortilla and place seam-side down on serving plates. Top with salsa and sour cream of choice.

MENU PLANNING TIPS

This fajita features the flavor of grilled vegetables. Serve topped with Thick and Chunky Salsa *(p. 125)* or purchased salsa, and Tofu Sour Cream *(p. 122)* or nonfat sour cream.

TAMALE PIE

Serves 8
Prep. time: 10 minutes
Cooking time: 75 minutes

1	15-ounce can whole-kernel corn
1	15-ounce creamed corn
1	28-ounce can stewed tomatoes
1	28-ounce can tomato purée
1	can pitted olives, sliced
1	4-ounce can green chilies, chopped (optional)
3	cups uncooked cornmeal
6	teaspoons cornstarch
2	tablespoons granulated onions *or* onion powder
3	teaspoons salt
3	tablespoons honey *or* sugar
½	cup tofu *or* soy milk powder *or* powdered nondairy creamer
2	tablespoons oil

1. Mix all ingredients together in large mixing bowl. Put mixture in large roasting pan that has been sprayed with nonstick cooking spray. Place in oven at 450°F for 30 minutes.

2. Change oven temperature to 375°F and continue baking for 30 minutes, then cover with aluminum foil and bake an additional 15 minutes, or until cornmeal is completely cooked. Mixture becomes thick. Serve warm.

NO-GUILT REFRIED BEANS

Serves 4
Prep. time: 10 minutes
Cooking time: 10 minutes

MENU PLANNING TIPS

Serve with tacos, burritos, or chips. This is a great side dish, or an ingredient for many recipes. There is no added fat in these beans. I sometimes use this recipe with my Layered Bean Dip *(p. 97)* to replace the beans.

1	16-ounce can pinto beans, rinsed and drained
¼	cup Thick and Chunky Salsa *(p. 125)*
2	tablespoons onion, chopped, *or* ½ tablespoon onion powder
¼	teaspoon garlic powder
¼-½	teaspoon ground cumin (optional)
¼	teaspoon chili powder (optional)

1. In 2-quart saucepan over medium-high heat, combine beans, salsa, onion, garlic powder, cumin, and chili powder. Bring mixture to a boil, stirring occasionally.

2. Reduce heat to medium-low. Simmer 7 to 10 minutes, or until onion is translucent, stirring occasionally.

3. In food processor or blender, process mixture until smooth.

MAZIDRA

2	tablespoons olive oil
1-2	large onions, chopped
8	ounces dried lentils, sorted and rinsed
6-8	garlic cloves, thinly sliced *or* minced
5	cups water
1	teaspoon salt *or* to taste
1	teaspoon McKay's Chicken-Style Seasoning *or* Chicken-like Seasoning *(p. 121)*

1. In large saucepan over medium-high heat, combine olive oil and onions. Cook about 3 minutes, then add dried lentils. Cook 5 minutes, stirring constantly. Add garlic and cook an additional 5 minutes, stirring constantly. The lentils will brown slightly on the outside but should be able to be cut in half easily. The lentils are cooked just enough if a lentil breaks in half easily when you bite it.

2. Add water, salt, and McKay's Chicken-Style Seasoning or Chicken-like Seasoning and bring to a boil. Lower heat and simmer, covered, for about 30 minutes, or until lentils are tender. The lentils will not get as soft or mushy using this cooking technique. They have a nuttier flavor and texture. Serve on the side of rice, over rice, over baked potatoes, or over couscous.

INDIAN LENTILS AND RICE

1/2	cup green onions, chopped
1	tablespoon ginger, finely chopped
2-4	garlic cloves, minced
5 1/4	cups water
5	teaspoons McKay's Chicken-Style Seasoning *or* any vegetable seasoning
1 1/2	cups dried lentils, sorted and rinsed
1	teaspoon ground turmeric
1/2	teaspoon salt
1	large tomato, chopped
1/4	cup shredded coconut
2	tablespoons fresh mint leaves *or* 2 teaspoons dried mint leaves
3	cups hot cooked rice
1 1/2	cups Tofu Yogurt *(p. 117)* *or* fat-free plain yogurt

1. Spray 3-quart saucepan with nonstick cooking spray. Cook onions, grated ginger, and garlic in saucepan over medium heat for 3 to 5 minutes, stirring occasionally, until onions are tender.

2. Stir in 5 cups of water and McKay's Chicken-Style Seasoning or vegetable seasoning, lentils, turmeric, and salt. Heat to boiling; reduce heat. Cover and simmer about 25 to 30 minutes, adding remaining water, if needed, until lentils are tender. Stir in tomato, coconut, and mint. Serve over rice with yogurt.

Serves 6-8
Prep. time: 10 minutes
Cooking time: 30-40 minutes

MENU PLANNING TIPS

This dish features lentils with a flavor like no other lentil dish I've ever made. The dried lentils are sautéed with the onion, garlic, and olive oil, and they soak up that flavor. They maintain a crispy outside and a soft inside, changing the flavor of the lentils totally. Try this dish with rice, baked potatoes, or couscous.

Serves 6
Prep. time: 10 minutes
Cooking time: 30 minutes

MENU PLANNING TIPS

Try this Indian dish that features lentils seasoned with gingerroot and mint. Serve over rice, topped with yogurt.

Main Dish Dinner

PIZZA

Roasted Vegetable Pizza

Quick Pizza Dough

Spinach-Pesto Salad Pizza

Grilled Vegetable Pizza With
Spinach-Walnut Pesto

Pesto Pizza

Fresh Tomato-Herb Pizza

Herbed Pizza Crust

French Bread Pizza With Beans
and Chunky Vegetables

OASTED VEGETABLE PIZZA

Serves 6
Prep. time: 20 minutes
Cooking time: 30 minutes

1	tablespoon fresh *or* 1 teaspoon dried thyme leaves
2	tablespoons lemon juice
1	teaspoon olive oil
$\frac{1}{4}$	teaspoon salt
4	small red potatoes, each cut into eight wedges
4	garlic cloves, thinly sliced
1	small yellow summer squash, cut into $\frac{1}{4}$-inch slices
1	small red bell pepper, cut into 2-inch pieces
1	small sweet onion, cut into twelve wedges
$1\frac{1}{4}$	cups Cheeseless "Cheese" Sauce *(p. 127)* *or* grated low-fat cheddar cheese
1	10-inch pizza crust, purchased *or* prepared from Herbed Pizza Crust *(p. 107)*, baked according to directions

1. Preheat oven to 500°F.

2. Combine thyme and remaining ingredients (except cheese and crust) in a bowl; toss well. Place vegetable mixture in 13" x 9" baking dish. Bake at 500°F for 15 minutes, stirring halfway through cooking time. Remove from oven.

3. Reduce oven temperature to 425°F. Sprinkle half of the cheese over prepared pizza crust. Arrange roasted vegetables over cheese, and top with remaining cheese. Bake at 425°F for 12 minutes, or until crust is lightly browned.

UICK PIZZA DOUGH

Makes 1 crust
Prep. time: 15 minutes
Cooking time: 10-15 minutes

MENU PLANNING TIPS
This easy-to-make pizza dough can be used as the crust for the pizza of your choice.

$1\frac{1}{2}$	cups all-purpose flour
$\frac{1}{2}$	cup whole-wheat flour
1	tablespoon quick-rising yeast
1	teaspoon salt
$\frac{1}{2}$	teaspoon sugar *or* honey
1	teaspoon olive oil
$\frac{3}{4}$	cup water

1. In a food processor, combine flours, yeast, salt, and honey or sugar; pulse to mix.

2. In a small saucepan or glass measuring cup, mix oil with water and heat in microwave to 125°F to 130°F. With the processor on, gradually pour the warm liquid through the feed tube. (If the mixture is too dry, add 1 or 2 tablespoons more warm water.) Process until the dough forms a ball, then process for 1 minute to knead.

3. Transfer the dough to a lightly floured surface. Cover with plastic wrap and let rest for 10 to 15 minutes.

4. On a floured surface, use a rolling pin to roll pizza dough out to a circle that's about 12 inches in diameter and $\frac{1}{2}$ inch in thickness. Transfer the dough to a pizza pan or a circular bake stone that has been lightly coated with cornmeal. (This prevents the crust from sticking to pan.)

5. Bake in 425°F oven for 12 to 15 minutes, or until lightly browned.

SPINACH-PESTO SALAD PIZZA

SPINACH-PESTO SALAD PIZZA

4	6-inch pizza crusts, purchased *or* prepared from Herbed Pizza Crust *(p. 107)*, unbaked
1	teaspoon olive oil *or* 1 tablespoon water
1	18-ounce can Loma Linda Tender Bits, sliced
	or
10	ounces firm tofu, sautéed until browned, seasoned with garlic powder *and/or* McKay's Chicken-Style Seasoning *or* Chicken-like Seasoning *(p. 121)*
½	red pepper, sliced into thin, 1½-inch-long strips
1	green onion, sliced
½	cup Basil-Pine Nut Pesto *(p. 124)*
6	firm-ripe Roma tomatoes, chopped
2	cups (3 ounces) firmly packed spinach leaves, rinsed and drained, cut into fine slivers
2	tablespoons lemon juice
4	tablespoons pine nuts for tossing *or* garnishing

1. Place crusts in a single layer on a 12- to 15-inch baking sheet. Bake in a 350°F oven until browned and crisp, about 15 minutes.
2. In nonstick skillet over medium heat, cook Tender Bits or tofu, red peppers, and green onions in olive oil or water until peppers are tender.
3. Prepare Basil-Pine Nut Pesto.
4. Toss well the tomatoes, spinach, pesto, and lemon juice, evenly coating the vegetables with pesto sauce. Add additional 4 tablespoons of pine nuts and mix well.
5. Place crusts on dinner plates. Top crusts with equal amounts of spinach-pesto mixture. Serve immediately.

Serves 4
Prep. time: 15 minutes
Cooking time: 15 minutes

MENU PLANNING TIPS

This salad pizza is so easy to prepare and so delicious! This is definitely a dish that family and guests are sure to enjoy. Keep purchased pizza crusts on hand, and you can toss this dinner together in no time.

GRILLED VEGETABLE PIZZA WITH SPINACH-WALNUT PESTO

1	12-inch pizza crust, baked
2	small zucchini, sliced lengthwise into ½-inch-thick sticks
2	vine-ripened tomatoes, seeded and chopped (2 cups)
1	tablespoon walnut *or* olive oil
½	teaspoon garlic powder
½	teaspoon onion powder
2	tablespoons Cheeseless "Parmesan" Cheese *(p. 127)* *or* fresh Parmesan cheese

1. In a mixing bowl, toss zucchini and tomatoes in oil and season with garlic powder and onion powder. Place vegetables on a baking sheet and bake at 500°F for 8 to 10 minutes, or until tender and browned.
2. Prepare the Spinach-Walnut Pesto *(p. 125)*.
3. To assemble the pizza: Spread the pizza crust with the pesto and distribute the vegetable mixture over the top of it. Just before serving, sprinkle with Parmesan cheese of choice.

Serves 6-8
Prep. time: 20 minutes
Cooking time: 10 minutes

MENU PLANNING TIPS

This pizza is flavored with a delicious crust, pesto, and grilled vegetables. If the crust is made ahead, this recipe can be put together very quickly. Serve with your choice of pizza crust.

PESTO PIZZA

Serves 8
Prep. time: 10 minutes
Cooking time: 15 minutes

1	cup mushrooms, sliced
1	large red onion, chopped
1	green bell pepper, chopped
1	large tomato, seeded and chopped
1	teaspoon lemon juice
1	teaspoon sugar *or* honey
1	12-inch pizza crust, purchased *or* prepared from Herbed Pizza Crust *(p.107)*, baked according to directions
2	teaspoons olive oil
$^1/_2$	cup feta cheese, crumbled, *or* tofu cheese, grated (optional)

PESTO SAUCE:

2	cups fresh basil leaves
4	peeled garlic cloves
1	tablespoon olive oil
3	tablespoons pine nuts
$^1/_4$	teaspoon salt
$^1/_4$	teaspoon McKay's Chicken-Style Seasoning *or* Chicken-like Seasoning *(p. 121)* (optional)

1. Purée all pesto sauce ingredients in food processor until smooth.
2. Spray nonstick cooking spray into nonstick skillet; heat skillet at medium-high temperature. Add mushrooms, onion, and pepper; sauté until vegetables are tender. Add tomato, and cook until tomato is warmed. (For saucier topping, cook tomato longer.) Add lemon juice and sugar or honey.
3. Brush pizza crust with olive oil and pesto sauce. Arrange vegetables on top of pizza. Top with cheese. Place on baking sheet or pizza stone. Heat for 10 to 15 minutes, or until lightly browned. Cut into eight wedges; serve hot.

FRESH TOMATO-HERB PIZZA

Serves 8
Prep. time: 20 minutes
Cooking time: 15 minutes

2	12-inch pizza crusts, purchased *or* prepared from Herbed Pizza Crust *(p. 107)*, unbaked
1	teaspoon oil
$^3/_4$	cup onion, chopped
2	garlic cloves, minced
$4^1/_2$	cups plum tomatoes, chopped
2	cups yellow tomatoes, chopped (substitute with more red plum tomatoes)
$^1/_2$	teaspoon salt (optional)
1- 2	cups Cheeseless "Cheese" Sauce *(p. 127)* *or* grated low-fat mozzarella cheese
2	tablespoons fresh basil, chopped, *or* 2 teaspoons dried basil, crushed
2	tablespoons fresh oregano, chopped, *or* 2 teaspoons dried oregano, crushed

Fresh Tomato Herb Pizza, continued

1. Heat 1 teaspoon oil in nonstick skillet over medium-high heat. Add onion and garlic; sauté 3 minutes, or until tender. Remove from heat; stir in plum tomatoes and salt.

2. Preheat oven to 450°F and place unbaked pizza crusts on baking sheet or pizza stone for assembly.

3. Nondairy option: Prepare Cheeseless "Cheese" Sauce. Spread half of cheese sauce over each crust, then divide the plum tomato mixture between the two pizzas, leaving ½-inch border. Divide yellow tomatoes evenly between pizzas.

LOW-FAT DAIRY OPTION:

Spread plum tomato mixture evenly over prepared crusts, leaving a ½-inch border. Divide yellow tomatoes evenly between pizzas, and sprinkle each pizza with 1 cup of low-fat cheese.

4. Bake at 450°F for 12 to 15 minutes, or until lightly browned. Remove pizzas to cutting boards; let stand 5 minutes. Sprinkle each pizza with 1 tablespoon fresh basil and 1 tablespoon fresh oregano; slice and serve.

HERBED PIZZA CRUST

1	tablespoon honey
1	package (1⅓ tablespoons) active dry yeast
1	cup warm water (105°F to 115°F)
2½	cups all-purpose flour *or* whole-wheat flour
½	cup yellow cornmeal
1	tablespoon fresh thyme, chopped
1	teaspoon fresh rosemary, chopped
½	teaspoon fresh oregano, chopped
¼	teaspoon salt
2	teaspoons olive oil
2	tablespoons cornmeal

Makes two 12-inch crusts
Prep. time: 60 minutes
Cooking time: 10-12 minutes

MENU PLANNING TIPS
Use as the crust for any of the pizza recipes in this section. Top with any combination of toppings, as you would for traditional pizza. For variety, try adding fresh garlic cloves (minced or thinly sliced), sun-dried tomatoes, basil, or other herbs to this pizza crust.

1. Dissolve honey and yeast in warm water in a small bowl; let stand 5 minutes.

2. Place flour, ½ cup cornmeal, thyme, rosemary, oregano, and salt in a food processor; pulse 2 times, or until blended. With processor on, slowly add yeast and water mixture and 2 teaspoons of oil through food chute. Process until dough leaves sides of bowl and forms ball. Process 1 additional minute.

3. Turn dough onto a lightly floured surface and knead for 2 minutes. Place dough in a large bowl, coated with nonstick cooking spray, turning dough to coat top. Cover dough and let rise in a warm place (85°F), free from drafts, for 1 hour, or until doubled in bulk. (For small amounts of dough, I use the microwave with the door closed.)

4. Punch down risen dough and divide in half. Roll each half of dough into a 12-inch circle on a lightly floured surface. Place divided dough on two 12-inch pizza pans, baking sheets, or baking stones that are coated with nonstick cooking spray and sprinkled with 1 tablespoon cornmeal. Crimp edges of dough with fingers to form a rim around the edge.

5. Bake in preheated oven at 425°F for 10 to 12 minutes if recipe calls for a precooked crust. In some pizza recipes the toppings are added directly to the unbaked pizza dough and both are baked together. Consult recipes before baking the plain crust.

FRENCH BREAD PIZZA WITH BEANS AND CHUNKY VEGETABLES

CRUST:

4   5-inch-long pieces of French *or* Italian bread

TOPPING:

2   cups chunky vegetable tomato sauce, purchased, *or* Chunky Vegetable Sauce *(p. 64)*

1   15½-ounce can pinto *or* cannellini (white kidney) beans, drained and rinsed

½   small red onion, halved and thinly sliced

2-4   tablespoons fresh basil, chopped, *or* ½ teaspoon dried basil

⅛   teaspoon garlic powder

2   cups Cheeseless "Cheese" Sauce *(p. 127) or* grated, reduced-fat, part-skim mozzarella cheese

fresh chopped basil for garnish

Serves 8
Prep. time: 15 minutes
Cooking time: 12-15 minutes

1.   Preheat oven to 425°F. Line a large cookie sheet with foil; spray with nonstick cooking spray.

2.   Cut each piece of bread in half horizontally. Hollow out center of each to form ¾-inch-thick shell. Save bread crumbs for another use. If necessary, cut thin slice off rounded bottom of each piece so it will sit firmly while baking. Place on cookie sheet, hollowed side up. Set aside.

3.   In large bowl, combine Chunky Vegetable Sauce, beans, onion, basil, and garlic powder; mix well. Divide mixture evenly among shells, spreading almost to edges. Spoon cheese sauce over tomato layer, or sprinkle with grated cheese. Top cheese layer with additional chopped fresh basil, if desired.

4.   Bake at 425°F for 15 minutes, until cheese sauce is bubbly or the sprinkled cheese is melted and lightly browned, and the filling is hot.

Dessert

Peanut Butter Cookies

Glazed Fresh Strawberry Pie

Pumpkin Pie

Blueberry Crisp

Fresh Apple-Pineapple
Cream Pie

Glazed Fresh Peach Pie

Pastry Crust

Low-Fat Raspberry
Cheesecake

Strawberry-Almond Torte

PEANUT BUTTER COOKIES

1	cup applesauce
1/4	cup canola oil
1	banana
1	cup peanut butter
1	cup brown sugar
1	cup all-purpose flour *or* whole-wheat flour
1/2	teaspoon salt
2	tablespoons water
2 1/2	cups all-purpose flour *or* whole-wheat flour
2	teaspoons baking soda
6	tablespoons cornstarch

1. Place applesauce, oil, and banana in blender or food processor and process until smooth and slightly foamy. Place in large mixing bowl.
2. Add peanut butter, brown sugar, 1 cup flour, salt, and water. Mix well.
3. Add additional flour, baking soda, and cornstarch. Mix well.
4. Place cookie dough by rounded teaspoonfuls on ungreased cookie sheet. Dip fork in water and flatten each mound of cookie dough to form a cookie that's approximately 1/2 inch in thickness.
5. Bake at 325°F for 12 to 15 minutes, or until top is light brown. Edges and bottoms should be golden brown, and the centers should still be slightly soft. When cookies cool, they will get harder, so if you like soft cookies, undercook them slightly. If you like crispy cookies, cook the full 15 minutes.

Makes:
five dozen 2 1/2-inch cookies
Prep. time: 10 minutes
Cooking time: 12-15 minutes

RECIPE TIPS

This cookie recipe contains no milk, eggs, or shortening. Applesauce and a banana replace the shortening. Crunchy peanut butter can be used if you like peanut pieces in your cookies. You can replace brown sugar with 1 cup honey and add to liquid mixture in blender, processing until smooth and foamy. Delete water if using honey.

GLAZED FRESH STRAWBERRY PIE

1	9-inch Pastry Crust *(p. 115)*, baked
6	cups fresh strawberries, hulled
1	cup water
2	tablespoons cornstarch
2	tablespoons cool water
1/4	cup sugar *or* honey
	red food coloring *or* grape juice for color (optional)

1. Prepare Pastry Crust according to directions.
2. Place 1 cup of strawberries and 1 cup of water in food processor or blender. Cover and process or blend till mixture is smooth. Transfer to a small saucepan. Bring to a boil; simmer 2 minutes.
3. Whisk together cornstarch and 2 tablespoons water until cornstarch is dissolved. Add honey or sugar. Stir into blended berry mixture. Cook and stir over medium heat till mixture is thickened and bubbly. Cook and stir 2 minutes more. Remove from heat. Stir in red food coloring or grape juice to tint a rich red color. Cool to room temperature.
4. Fold remaining fresh strawberries into cooled sauce mixture. Pour into baked pie shell. Cover and chill for 3 to 4 hours or until set. Serve garnished with nondairy whipped topping of choice.

Serves 8
Prep. time: 10 minutes
Cooking time: 15 minutes

RECIPE TIPS

If you prefer, you can delete the water and sugar or honey and use apple juice concentrate as you would the water. The juice provides the liquid and the sweetener for the pie. Garnish with nondairy whipped topping or Tofu Whipped Cream *(p. 122)*.

PUMPKIN PIE

Serves 16
Makes two 9-inch pies
Prep. time: 10 minutes
Cooking time: 80 minutes

RECIPE TIPS

No one will even notice that the eggs and milk have been replaced with more nutritious ingredients. Serve with nondairy whipped topping or Tofu Whipped Cream *(p. 122)*.

2	uncooked Pastry Crusts *(p. 115)*
1	29-ounce can Libby's pumpkin
4	tablespoons cornstarch
¾	cup water
1½	cups sugar
1	teaspoon salt
2	teaspoons cinnamon
1	teaspoon ginger
1	teaspoon cloves
½	cup Soyagen (soy milk powder) *or* nondairy creamer powder
2½	cups water
1	cup all-purpose flour

1. Preheat oven to 425°F.
2. Empty can of pumpkin into large mixing bowl.
3. In small bowl, whisk together cornstarch and cool water until cornstarch is dissolved. Add to pumpkin and mix well. Add ¾ cup water, sugar, salt, cinnamon, ginger, and cloves. Mix well.
4. Mix together milk powder of choice and 2½ cups water until dissolved. Add to pumpkin mixture. Mix well. Add flour and mix.
5. Pour pumpkin mixture into two 9-inch pie shells. If baking both pies at once, place one pie on bottom rack of oven and one on top rack, and place aluminum foil loosely over each pie. Halfway through baking time, exchange the pies' oven position. If baking only one pie, place it on lower rack and place foil over top rack to prevent the crust and pie top from overbrowning. Bake for 15 minutes at 425°F, then lower the temperature to 350°F for the remaining time. For the last 10 minutes, remove the foil and lightly brown piecrust.

BLUEBERRY CRISP

Serves 10
Prep. time: 10 minutes
Cooking time: 40 minutes

RECIPE TIPS

This recipe can be made with your choice of fruits and topped with the delicious crisp topping. Serve with nondairy whipped topping or Tofu Whipped Cream *(p. 122)*.

1	12-ounce can frozen apple juice concentrate, undiluted
2	tablespoons cornstarch
1	tablespoon margarine (optional)
1	teaspoon lemon juice
1	teaspoon cinnamon
6	cups fresh *or* frozen blueberries

CRUMB TOPPING:

¼	cup canola oil
⅓	cup honey
½	cup pecans, chopped
½	cup all-purpose *or* whole-wheat flour
2	cups quick-cooking oats

Blueberry Crisp, continued

1. In large saucepan or skillet, combine thawed apple juice concentrate and cornstarch; whisk together until completely dissolved. Cook over medium heat until thickened. Add margarine, lemon juice, and cinnamon. Stir to blend ingredients. Remove mixture from heat, pour over blueberries, and toss well.

2. To prepare crumb topping: In medium-size mixing bowl, cream together oil and honey. Add chopped nuts, flour, and oats. Toss well, coating all dry ingredients with the oil-and-honey mixture.

3. In 9" x 13" baking dish sprayed with nonstick cooking spray, place the blueberry filling. Sprinkle crumb topping evenly over the fruit. Bake in 350°F oven for 30 to 40 minutes, or until crumb topping is golden brown and the filling is bubbling. Serve warm with whipped topping of choice.

RESH APPLE-PINEAPPLE CREAM PIE

1   9-inch Pastry Crust *(p. 115)*, baked
5   large Golden Delicious apples, grated

NONDAIRY OPTION:

1½   cups firm tofu
1-2   tablespoons canola oil
1   tablespoon lemon juice
¼-½   teaspoon lemon rind, grated
2-4   tablespoons honey
1   teaspoon vanilla
½   teaspoon salt
1   16-ounce can crushed pineapple, slightly drained

DAIRY OPTION:

2   cups nonfat pineapple yogurt
1   16-ounce can crushed pineapple, drained

1. Prepare Pastry Crust according to directions.

2. For nondairy option: Blend the tofu, oil, lemon juice, lemon rind, honey, vanilla, and salt until smooth and creamy. If mixture is too thick to blend, add pineapple juice from the canned pineapple one tablespoon at a time to make mixture blendable. Stir in canned pineapple and grated apples.

   For dairy option: Mix together purchased nonfat pineapple yogurt, canned pineapple, and grated apple.

3. Pour pie filling into cooled pastry crust. Cover and chill approximately 2 hours to set.

Serves 8
Prep. time: 10 minutes
Cooking time: 10-12 minutes

RECIPE TIPS

You can use any flavor yogurt to change the flavor of this pie. The tofu pie filling can also be made with your choice of fresh fruits added for variety in flavor. Garnish with nondairy whipped topping or Tofu Whipped Cream *(p. 122)* and slivered almonds just before serving.

GLAZED FRESH PEACH PIE

1   9-inch Pastry Crust *(recipe below)*, baked

6   cups fresh peaches, pitted, peeled, and cut in wedges

1   cup water

2   tablespoons cornstarch

2   tablespoons cool water

¼   cup sugar *or* honey

1. Prepare Pastry Crust according to directions. To make the checkerboard edge, as shown, use a sharp knife to cut across the rim at ½-inch intervals. Fold every other piece in toward the center.

2. Place 1 cup peaches and 1 cup water in food processor or blender. Cover and process or blend till mixture is smooth. Transfer to a small saucepan. Bring to a boil; simmer 2 minutes.

3. Whisk together cornstarch and 2 tablespoons water until cornstarch is dissolved. Add honey or sugar. Stir into peach mixture. Cook and stir over medium heat till mixture is thickened and bubbly. Cook and stir 2 minutes more. Remove from heat. Cool to room temperature.

4. Fold remaining fresh peaches into cooled sauce mixture. Turn into baked pie shell. Cover and chill for 3 to 4 hours or until set.

PASTRY CRUST

1¼   cups all-purpose flour

¼   teaspoon salt

⅓   cup canola oil

4   tablespoons cold water

1. Sift flour and salt. Whisk cold water into oil until emulsified. Pour oil mixture into dry mixture. Stir quickly with fork until flour is coated with oil mixture. To prevent a tough crust, be careful not to handle pastry dough too much.

2. Roll out pastry dough between two pieces of waxed paper until it is 2 inches larger than the diameter of the pie plate you are using. Peel off the top piece of waxed paper and lay rolled pastry over the pie or tart pan. Remove waxed paper and fit crust into the pan, removing all air bubbles. Finish the edge according to your preference. If using a tart pan, use your fingers to seal the top edge of crust tightly to the pan to keep crust from falling in as it bakes.

3. If you are baking the crust without a filling, be sure to prick the bottom and sides of the uncooked crust liberally with a fork to prevent air bubbles and falling edges. Bake in 450°F oven for 12 to 15 minutes, or till pastry is golden. Cool on a wire rack.

Dessert

Serves 8
Prep. time: 10 minutes
Cooking time: 10-12 minutes

RECIPE TIPS

This recipe is a delicious presentation of fresh peaches. You can use blueberries or any other fresh fruit with this glaze. If you prefer, you can delete the water and sugar or honey and use apple juice concentrate as you would the water. The juice provides the liquid and the sweetener for the pie. Garnish with nondairy whipped topping or Tofu Whipped Cream *(p. 122)*.

Makes 1 crust
Prep. time: 5 minutes
Cooking time: 12-15 minutes

RECIPE TIPS

Options for crust: You can decrease flour by 2 tablespoons and replace it with toasted wheat germ. This works well when using the crust for a main dish recipe. If baking the crust without filling, decrease the oil by 1 tablespoon. If you like a thicker crust, you can layer this piecrust by rolling out one crust and then placing another rolled-out crust directly on top of the first one. This also makes a great top crust for hearty pot-pies or fruit pies.

LOW-FAT RASPBERRY CHEESECAKE

1	cup fresh *or* loose-pack frozen raspberries
1	cup all-purpose flour *or* whole-wheat flour
1	teaspoon baking powder
½	cup sugar *or* honey
¼	cup canola oil
1	tablespoon cornstarch
3	tablespoons water
1	teaspoon vanilla
1	cup plain fat-free yogurt *or* Tofu Yogurt (below)
¼	cup sugar *or* honey
1	tablespoon cornstarch
3	tablespoons water
2	tablespoons all-purpose flour
1½	teaspoons lemon peel, finely shredded
1	teaspoon vanilla

Serves 12
Prep. time: 15 minutes
Cooking time: 35 minutes

RECIPE TIP
Serve with Tofu Yogurt (below).

1. Spray a 9-inch springform pan with nonstick cooking spray; set aside. Thaw frozen raspberries at room temperature for 15 minutes. Drain, if necessary.

2. Combine flour, baking powder, and sugar (if using sugar).

3. In separate mixing bowl, combine oil and honey (if using instead of sugar). In small cup, whisk 1 tablespoon cornstarch into 3 tablespoons water. Add the cornstarch mixture to the oil mixture. Add 1 teaspoon vanilla and mix well. Combine flour mixture with liquid mixture. Spread onto bottom of prepared pan; sprinkle with loose raspberries.

4. Combine the yogurt of choice, ¼ cup sugar or honey, 1 tablespoon cornstarch, 3 tablespoons water, 2 tablespoons flour, lemon peel, and 1 teaspoon vanilla in medium mixing bowl. Mix till smooth; pour over berries-and-cream mixture.

5. Bake in a 350°F oven about 45 to 50 minutes, or until center appears set when shaken gently. Cool in pan on a wire rack for 15 minutes. Loosen and remove sides of pan. Cool completely. Cover and chill for 2 to 24 hours before serving.

TOFU YOGURT:

1	cup firm tofu
2	tablespoons canola oil
1	tablespoon lemon juice
1½	teaspoons honey
1	teaspoon vanilla
½	teaspoon salt

Makes 1¼ cups

Combine all ingredients in a blender or food processor. Blend until smooth and creamy. Chill until serving.

STRAWBERRY-ALMOND TORTE

CRUST INGREDIENTS:

¼	cup canola oil
¼-½	cup sugar *or* honey
2	egg whites *or* 2 tablespoons cornstarch, mixed with 6 tablespoons water
1	teaspoon vanilla
2	cups all-purpose *or* whole-wheat flour
¼	teaspoon salt
¼	cup almonds, thinly sliced *or* chopped (optional)

ALMOND FILLING FOR CRUST:

2	egg whites *or* 2 tablespoons cornstarch, mixed with 6 tablespoons water
¼	cup sugar *or* honey
½	teaspoon almond extract
1	teaspoon pure vanilla extract
½	cup almond paste (available in specialty section of grocery store)

WHIPPED TOPPING:

4	cups 1 percent tofu, soft
½	cup canola oil
½	cup honey
2	teaspoons lemon juice
½	teaspoon salt
6	teaspoons vanilla
	or
4	cups nondairy whipped topping *(as substitute for tofu whipped topping)*

FRESH FRUIT FILLING:

1	quart fresh strawberries

1. To make crust: Whisk together oil and honey or sugar until frothy. Add egg whites or cornstarch and water mixture to the oil/honey mixture and whisk again. (Be sure cornstarch is well dissolved in the water before adding to oil mixture.) Add vanilla and mix well. Stir in flour, salt, and almonds. Divide crust ingredients and spread into two 9-inch round pans, half in each pan. Set aside. Preheat oven to 350°F.

2. To make almond filling: Beat egg whites or water and cornstarch until foamy. Gradually add sugar or honey, vanilla, and almond extract and beat together well. Blend in the almond paste and mix well. Spread half of filling on top of each uncooked crust.

3. Bake crust with almond filling at 350°F for 25 to 30 minutes. Cool 5 minutes before removing from the pans. Turn over pans to remove crust and let cool on cooling racks.

4. To make whipped topping: Blend all ingredients—tofu, oil, honey, lemon juice, salt, and vanilla—until smooth and creamy. Chill until serving.

5. To prepare fresh strawberry filling: Wash and stem the berries and leave half of the nicest looking ones whole for the top of the torte. Cut the rest of the berries in half to be used in the center of the torte.

6. To assemble the torte: Place one of the cooled crusts on a cake plate. Spread with half the whipped topping. Place the halved strawberries on top of the whipped topping. Top with the remaining crust. Spread the top of the crust with the remaining whipped topping. Top with the whole strawberries, turned stem-side down, placed closely together so that they cover the entire top of the crust. Serve immediately.

Serves 12
Prep. time: 20 minutes
Cooking time: 30 minutes

RECIPE TIPS

This recipe should be assembled just before serving. If you make this for company, prepare the crusts and have them cooled and ready for assembly. Make the whipped topping (below) and have it chilling in the refrigerator, or use purchased nondairy whipped topping. Wash and prepare the strawberries and chill until ready to serve. Having made these preparations, you can assemble the torte in 5 minutes. This prevents the crust from becoming soggy.

Many people on special diets because of allergies or illness may not be able to tolerate some spices or seasonings such as chili powder and vinegar. Others may be allergic to milk products or may be following a vegan vegetarian diet, eliminating these foods.

This section has nondairy options for mayonnaise, salad dressings, and cheeses. It also has substitutions for some of the seasonings and spices that are not tolerated by some people. There is even a ketchup recipe without vinegar. You'll love the pesto sauces that are made without cheese. Try these delicious substitutions and variations that will not leave you feeling deprived.

Variations & Substitutions

Cinnamon Substitute

Chili Powder Substitute

Chicken-like Seasoning

Tofu Whipped Cream

Tofu Yogurt or Sour Cream

Low-Fat Creamy Onion-Dill Dressing

Ranch Soy Mayonnaise

Nondairy Creamy Onion-Dill Dressing

Creamy Herb Dressing

Creamy Cucumber Dressing

Basil-Pine Nut Pesto

Spinach-Walnut Pesto

Thick and Chunky Salsa

Classic Fresh Salsa

Guacamole

Tartar Sauce

Sweet-and-Sour Sauce

Vinegar-free Tomato Ketchup

Cheeseless "Parmesan" Cheese

Cheeseless "Cheese" Sauce

INNAMON SUBSTITUTE

Use coriander seed in equal amounts to cinnamon, *or* use 1 part coriander seed and 1 part anise seed, *or* use 3 parts coriander seed and 1 part sweet anise seed. Grind to a powder in an electric Moulinex, or by hand with a mortar and pestle. Use in place of cinnamon.

CHILI POWDER SUBSTITUTE

Makes 6 tablespoons

1	tablespoon paprika
1	teaspoon cumin
2	bay leaves
1	tablespoon sweet basil
1	tablespoon dried bell pepper
1	tablespoon parsley flakes
1	teaspoon ground dillweed *or* ½ teaspoon dill seed
1	teaspoon oregano
1	tablespoon onion powder

Grind all ingredients to fine powder in an electric Moulinex, or by hand with mortar and pestle. Store in well-cleaned seasoning container.

CHICKEN-LIKE SEASONING

Makes ½ cup

⅓	cup nutritional yeast flakes
¾	teaspoon dried green bell pepper
¼-½	teaspoon salt
½	teaspoon dried celery flakes
½	teaspoon garlic powder
1	teaspoon onion powder
½	teaspoon sage
½	teaspoon thyme
¼	teaspoon marjoram
1	tablespoon parsley flakes

Mix ingredients and grind to a powder in an electric Moulinex, or by hand with mortar and pestle. Store in sealed container.

TOFU WHIPPED CREAM

Makes 1¹/₂ cups
Prep. time: 5 minutes

RECIPE TIPS
This whipped cream alternative contains no cholesterol or saturated fat. If you use firm tofu in this recipe, you will need to add a few tablespoons of water to thin the cream to a blendable consistency. This whipped cream can be made up to three days in advance and chilled until needed.

1	10-ounce container 1 percent tofu, soft
2	tablespoons canola oil *or* olive oil
2	tablespoons honey
¹/₂	teaspoon lemon juice
¹/₈	teaspoon salt
1¹/₂	teaspoons vanilla

Combine all ingredients in blender or food processor and process until smooth and creamy. Chill and serve as you would whipped cream.

TOFU YOGURT OR SOUR CREAM

Makes 1¹/₄ cups
Prep. time: 5 minutes

RECIPE TIPS
This nondairy alternative can be used whenever a recipe calls for yogurt or sour cream. It can be made ahead and chilled up to five days.

1	10-ounce container 1 percent tofu, soft
2	tablespoons canola oil
1	tablespoon lemon juice
1¹/₂	teaspoons honey
¹/₂	teaspoon salt

Combine all ingredients in blender or food processor and blend until smooth. Chill until serving.

LOW-FAT CREAMY ONION-DILL DRESSING

Makes approximately
¹/₂ cup

¹/₄	cup fat-free mayonnaise *or* salad dressing
¹/₄	cup fat-free plain yogurt *or* tofu yogurt
1	tablespoon lemon juice
¹/₄	teaspoon onion powder
2	green onions, thinly sliced (2 tablespoons) *or* 2 teaspoons chives, chopped
2	teaspoons fresh dill, chopped *or* ¹/₂ teaspoon dried dillweed

Combine all ingredients in small bowl. Cover and chill.

RANCH SOY MAYONNAISE

1	cup water
2/3	cup Soyagen (soy milk powder)
1	pinch salt (optional)
1	tablespoon honey *or* sugar
2-4	tablespoons Hidden Valley Ranch dressing mix
1/4	cup light olive oil *or* canola oil
	juice of 1 fresh lemon

1. In blender, place water, Soyagen,* salt, honey or sugar, and ranch dressing mix, and process until smooth.

2. While continuing to blend, slowly pour oil into mixture. Mixture will thicken. Pour into container that has sealable lid.

3. Stir lemon juice into mayonnaise mixture. The mayonnaise will thicken. Chill in sealed container until serving time.

If you do not have access to Soyagen, a soy milk powder, do not use any other soy or tofu milk powder, because the mayonnaise will not thicken. It is best to replace the water and Soyagen with 10 ounces of soft tofu, blended with enough water to thin to white-sauce consistency.

Makes 2 cups
Prep. time: 5 minutes

RECIPE TIPS

This soy mayonnaise tastes very much like the traditional ranch dressing. Use this recipe as a substitute for mayonnaise on sandwiches, topping for baked potatoes or vegetables, and for potato, chicken, or pasta salads. This mayonnaise contains no cholesterol.

NONDAIRY CREAMY ONION-DILL DRESSING

1/2	cup tofu, soft
2	tablespoons tofu *or* soy milk
2	tablespoons olive oil
2-3	teaspoons lemon juice
1	teaspoon honey
1/4	teaspoon salt
1/4	teaspoon garlic powder
1/4	teaspoon onion powder
2	green onions, thinly sliced (2 tablespoons), *or* 2 teaspoons chives, chopped
2	teaspoons fresh dill, chopped, *or* 1/2 teaspoon dried dillweed

1. Put all the above ingredients, except the green onions or chives and dill, in the blender and blend until smooth. Scrape sides of blender as needed.

2. Pour into bowl and stir in green onions or chives and dill. (Any fresh herb can be substituted for variety.) Add more lemon juice if a tangier taste is preferred. Cover and chill.

Makes 1 cup

RECIPE TIPS

This recipe makes a thick dip that is like a sour cream-based onion dip. It's great served with baked potatoes, potato skins, potato salad, and even can be used as a spread on bread. Thin it with more milk, to the consistency of French dressing, when using it in recipes such as Vegetable Potato Salad *(p. 90)* and Cheesy Potato Skins *(p. 91)*.

CREAMY HERB DRESSING

Makes 1 cup
Prep. time: 5 minutes

RECIPE TIPS
This dressing can be made thinner so it is pourable, or thicker if used for a dip. It can be made with any variety of herbs, preferably fresh herbs for the best flavor.

$1/2$	cup 1 percent tofu, soft
2	tablespoons tofu *or* soy *or* nonfat milk
2	tablespoons olive oil
2-3	tablespoons lemon juice
1	teaspoon honey
$1/4$	teaspoon salt
$1/4$	teaspoon garlic powder
2	teaspoons fresh dill *or* $1/2$-1 teaspoon dried dill

1. Combine all ingredients except the dill in the blender and blend until smooth. Scrape the sides of the blender as needed. Add more milk as needed to get a consistency that is quite thin and pourable.

2. Pour into bowl and stir in dill. Add more lemon juice if a tangier taste is preferred.

CREAMY CUCUMBER DRESSING

Makes 1½ cups
Prep. time: 5 minutes

RECIPE TIPS
Use this dressing with Middle Eastern dishes, Lentil Patties *(p. 42)*, or with any sandwiches or salads. Store in airtight container until serving.

$1/2$	cup tofu, soft
2	tablespoons tofu *or* soy *or* nonfat milk
2	tablespoons olive oil
2-3	teaspoons lemon juice
1	teaspoon honey
$1/4$	teaspoon salt
1	garlic clove, minced, *or* $1/4$ teaspoon garlic powder
2	teaspoons fresh dill *or* $1/2$-1 teaspoon dried dill
$1/4$	cucumber, peeled and grated, *or* chopped fine

1. Place the first seven ingredients in the blender and blend until smooth. Scrape sides of blender as needed. Add more milk as needed to get a consistency that is quite thin and pourable. A thinner consistency best blends the flavors of the food it's served with.

2. Pour into bowl and stir in dill and cucumber (fresh dill is preferred). Add more lemon juice if a tangier taste is preferred.

BASIL-PINE NUT PESTO

Makes 1 cup
Prep. time: 5 minutes

RECIPE TIPS
Use tossed into pasta, on pizza crust, garlic bread, salad greens, or on potatoes. If fresh basil is not available, use fresh spinach leaves or fresh parsley leaves, and then use 2 to 4 teaspoons dried basil.

$1/3$-$1/2$	cup fresh basil leaves
$1/3$	cup pine nuts
2	cloves garlic
$1/4$-$1/2$	cup olive oil
1	teaspoon lemon juice
$1/4$	teaspoon McKay's Chicken-Style Seasoning *or* Chicken-like Seasoning *(p. 121)* (optional)
	salt to taste (optional)

In blender or food processor combine basil leaves, nuts, and garlic cloves and process until finely chopped. Continue to scrape sides of container between blending. With machine running, pour in olive oil in a thin stream. Add lemon juice. Add McKay's Chicken-Style Seasoning and salt to taste, if desired. Process briefly until well mixed.

SPINACH-WALNUT PESTO

2	cups packed spinach leaves
2	tablespoons fresh basil leaves *or* 2 teaspoons dried basil
1/4	cup toasted walnuts
2-3	cloves garlic, peeled and chopped
1/4	cup nonfat yogurt *or* Tofu Yogurt *(p. 122)*
1	tablespoon walnut *or* olive oil
1/4	teaspoon lemon juice

1. Wash and prepare spinach leaves and fresh basil.
2. Toast walnuts in 350°F oven for 8 to 10 minutes.
3. In a food processor, combine spinach, basil, walnuts, and garlic. Pulse until very finely chopped. Add yogurt, oil, and lemon juice; process until smooth.

Makes 2 cups
Prep. time: 10 minutes

RECIPE TIPS
This delicious pesto is made with spinach leaves and basil. It is a great sauce tossed with pasta, served on garlic bread, pizza crust, potatoes, or salad.

THICK AND CHUNKY SALSA

3	14 1/2-ounce cans diced tomatoes
1	14 1/2-ounce can tomato sauce *or* purée
1	large onion, chopped
3-5	fresh jalapeño peppers, chopped (use less if you prefer milder salsa)
1/2	cup lemon juice
5	cloves garlic, minced
	salt to taste (optional)
1/2	bunch fresh cilantro, chopped

1. Place two cans of diced tomatoes in blender and process just a few seconds.
2. In medium-size saucepan, add partially blended tomatoes and the third can of diced tomatoes, tomato sauce or purée, onion, jalapeño peppers, lemon juice, garlic, and salt. Cook 10 to 20 minutes, or until salsa comes to a boil. Let cool. Add fresh cilantro. Place in sealed container and refrigerate until serving time.

Makes approximately
3 1/2 cups

CLASSIC FRESH SALSA

1 1/2	cups ripe tomatoes, chopped
1/4	cup green onions, sliced thin
2-4	tablespoons canned green chilies, chopped
1/4	cup fresh cilantro, chopped (optional)
1-1 1/2	teaspoons lemon juice
	salt to taste (optional)

Prepare vegetables and mix together. Serve chilled.

Makes 1 2/3 cups
Prep. time: 10 minutes

GUACAMOLE

Makes 1¼ cups

2	ripe avocados, peeled and pitted
1½	tablespoons fresh lime juice
¼	teaspoon garlic powder
¼	teaspoon salt (optional)
1	tablespoon fresh cilantro, chopped

In a bowl, coarsely mash avocados with a fork or pastry blender. Stir in lime juice, garlic powder, salt, and fresh cilantro.

TARTAR SAUCE

Makes 2½ cups

1	cup soft tofu, mashed
¼	cup lemon juice
2	tablespoons canola oil
2	tablespoons sugar *or* honey
¾	teaspoon dry mustard
¾	teaspoon salt
½	cup onion, chopped
¼	cup sweet pickle relish (optional)

1. In blender container, combine all ingredients except pickle relish and blend until smooth.
2. Fold in pickle relish. Chill until serving time.

SWEET-AND-SOUR SAUCE

Makes 2¾ cups

1½	cups unsweetened pineapple juice
½	cup plus 2 tablespoons brown sugar *or* molasses
	or
½	cup apple juice concentrate
½	cup lemon juice
½	teaspoon garlic powder
2	tablespoons cornstarch
¼	teaspoon soy sauce

1. In small saucepan, combine all the ingredients except cornstarch. Add cornstarch to cold sauce mixture and whisk until it is totally dissolved and no lumps remain.
2. Cook over medium heat, stirring constantly, until mixture is thickened.

INEGAR-FREE TOMATO KETCHUP

2 cups canned tomatoes, crushed, *or* 2 cups fresh tomatoes, diced

1 4-ounce can tomato paste

1/2 red bell pepper, chopped

1/4 cup onion, chopped

1/8 cup frozen orange juice concentrate

1 bay leaf

1/2 teaspoon celery seed

2 carrots, cut in chunks

4-6 tablespoons lemon juice, to taste

salt to taste (optional)

garlic powder to taste

1. In food processor, process all ingredients except the bay leaf until smooth and well blended.

2. Transfer mixture to small saucepan, add bay leaf, and simmer uncovered over medium-low heat, stirring constantly, to desired consistency. Add more orange and/or lemon juice to taste. If you prefer a sweeter flavor, add a small amount of honey or sugar. Remove bay leaf before serving.

HEESELESS "PARMESAN" CHEESE

1/2 cup nutritional yeast flakes

1/2 cup ground sesame seeds

2 teaspoons garlic powder

1 teaspoon onion powder

1 teaspoon McKay's Chicken-Style Seasoning *or* Chicken-like Seasoning *(p. 121)*

3 teaspoons lemon juice

Combine all ingredients except lemon juice in blender or food processor. Blend until all ingredients are finely ground. Add lemon juice and process until well blended. Store in refrigerator in airtight container.

HEESELESS "CHEESE" SAUCE

1 cup roasted cashews

1 cup water

1/2 cup pimientos *and/or* roasted red peppers

1/4 cup yeast flakes

1/4 cup sesame seeds

1/4 cup lemon juice

1/2-1 teaspoon salt

1 teaspoon onion powder

1/2 teaspoon garlic powder

Blend all the above ingredients until smooth. Use for Baked Enchilada Casserole *(p. 96)* or in the Layered Bean Dip recipe *(p. 97)*, or you can bake it in a casserole dish for 20 to 30 minutes, or until a knife inserted comes out clean. Use this baked Cheeseless "Cheese" as a dip for tortilla chips. Use it raw on top of pizza, for macaroni and cheese, lasagna, enchiladas, or other dishes that call for cheese and will be baked. The flavor is delicious.

NEW LABELS MAKE IT EASIER TO FOLLOW DIETARY GUIDELINES

It makes good sense to read the labels on the foods you buy, and now new labels make it easier to shop smart and eat right. Many food packages already display nutrition labels that follow new regulations set by the Food and Drug Administration (FDA). These labels give information that is more complete, accurate, and easy to understand, including the following:

SERVING SIZES

For the first time, serving sizes for similar foods must be consistent, making it easier to compare nutritional values.

1. **Total calories and calories from fat.** The label must show both calories per serving and the number of calories from fat, information you need to budget fat intake.

2. **Daily values for nutrients.** Given as percentages, daily values show the food's nutritional content, based on a daily diet of 2,000 calories.

3. **Calories per gram.** This information indicates how many calories are in each gram of fat, carbohydrate, and protein.

RECOMMENDED DIETARY GUIDELINES

The FDA recommends the following guidelines for an optimal diet that will aid in the prevention and treatment of chronic diseases.

Total fat:

No more than 30 percent of total calories per day.

Saturated fat:

No more than 10 percent of total calories per day.

Cholesterol:

No more than 300 milligrams per day.

Sodium:

No more than 2,400 milligrams per day.

Total carbohydrates:

A minimum of 55 percent of total calories per day.

Complex carbohydrates:

A minimum of 45 percent of total calories per day.

Fiber:

A minimum of 25 grams per day.

Protein:

12 to 15 percent of total calories per day.

A PEEK INTO MY PANTRY

Let's assume you've decided to make the transition to a healthful, plant-based diet. What foods do you need to buy? Where do you buy them? Which brands are best?

It isn't as overwhelming as it sounds. Let me show you what's in my pantry, refrigerator, freezer, and vegetable bin. If you begin to stock up on these items, you'll soon have all the supplies you need for the fix-it-fast, 30-minute meals in this book.

GRAINS

Oats:

Rolled oats and quick oats are used in this book. Rolled oats have a thicker flake and take longer to cook than quick oats.

Cornmeal:

Whole-grain is best, but most grocers sell only cornmeal that has the bran and germ removed. I like to use yellow cornmeal for the nice coloring it gives to food, but white cornmeal is equally nutritious.

Couscous:

Some call this the five-minute wonder. When it comes to speed, it doesn't get any better than instant couscous. Actually a form of pasta, couscous is made from golden semolina flour, mixed with water and rolled into tiny grains. Couscous is the national dish of Morocco, Tunisia, and Algeria. Whole-wheat couscous is becoming more common; if it's not at your supermarket, check a health food store.

Flour and Corn Tortillas:

Purchase these in the refrigerator or freezer section of the supermarket. They keep well when frozen.

Popcorn:

White hull-less is my favorite type of popcorn, because it has fewer hulls and is more tender than yellow popcorn.

Rice:

Short-grain rice has a sweeter taste and tends to hold together better. Long-grain rice does not stick together and has a richer taste.

Basmati Rice:

India's favorite rice is increasingly available in the United States and Canada, even in its unrefined state. This long-grain rice has a wonderful flavor and almost floral fragrance.

Millet:

Whole millet can be found in health food stores. It has much the same flavor as rice, but is, somehow, refreshingly different.

Whole-Wheat Flour:

I'm fortunate to have a kitchen mill for grinding my own flour. For breadmaking I use "hard" white winter-wheat berries for milling. They have a higher gluten content that produces the best quality whole-wheat bread. If you are purchasing your flour already milled, for the lightest bread choose a finely milled whole-wheat flour. For pastry or other nonyeast baked products, choose an all-purpose "soft" wheat flour. Its lower gluten content produces a more tender pastry. I keep all flours in the freezer to preserve their freshness and gluten content. (Be sure to bring the flour to room temperature before using it in baking.)

Wheat Gluten:

Small amounts added to yeast-activated baked goods improve volume, texture, and shelf life.

Enriched Unbleached White Flour:

I like to keep this on hand to combine with whole-wheat flour in some recipes.

Wheat Germ:

Available raw or toasted, this product is the heart of the wheat and adds a nutty flavor to many recipes. Toasted wheat germ has a longer shelf life and a nuttier flavor, but fewer nutrients than the raw. To maintain freshness, be sure to store raw wheat germ in the freezer.

Bulgur Wheat:

Available in health food stores and some supermarkets.

Pasta:

I stock a variety of pasta shapes and sizes, such as linguine, vermicelli, angel hair, ziti, egg noodles, spirals, shells, etc. The nutritional analysis for the pasta recipes in this book is based on the standard white noodle. For a higher fiber diet, replace white noodles with whole-wheat pasta.

NUTS AND SEEDS

Get nuts and seeds at the grocery store or health food store, or for a less-expensive source, investigate your local co-op. Buy them already roasted or purchase them raw and roast them yourself in a shallow pan in a 350°F oven for 5 to 10 minutes. To preserve their freshness, store large quantities of nuts and seeds in the freezer.

Almonds:

Raw, slivered, and sliced.

Cashews:

Unsalted, roasted.

Peanut Butter:

Be a label reader. Buy peanut butter that lists only peanuts and salt on the label—no added oils, sweeteners, or preservatives.

Pecans:

Raw, chopped.

Pine Nuts:

These are great when used in pasta with pesto, or on top of salads. They are also good when toasted in a 350°F oven for 5 to 10 minutes.

Sesame Seeds:

Hulled sesame seeds are white and have a milder flavor than the unhulled brown kind. Both are fine for cooking.

Tahini:

This is a sesame seed paste, or butter, made from ground unhulled sesame seeds. It is a common ingredient in many traditional Middle Eastern dishes. You can buy it in some grocery stores and most health food stores. Tahini will separate, so be sure to mix in the oils before each use. Refrigerate after opening.

Sunflower Seeds:

Buy these raw or dry-roasted.

Walnuts

LEGUMES

Most legumes are available either dried or canned. Use either kind in the recipes in this book. Canned beans are more convenient, but they're more expensive and may contain extra salt. They can be rinsed to lower the salt content.

Cannellini or White Kidney Beans:

These beans are an Italian bean that I use in many of my favorite recipes. They are more tender than regular kidney beans, and I love their flavor.

Garbanzos (Chickpeas)

Kidney Beans

Lentils

Pinto Beans

Red Beans

Tofu:

Tofu is made from soybean curd, just as cottage cheese is made from milk. It is a high-protein staple food for vegetarians that can be used to replace dairy and egg products in recipes. I prefer the Mori-Nu tofu, which is available in soft, firm, or extra firm, determined by how much liquid is left in the soy beans. It is also available in a lite (1 percent fat) version, and the flavor is the same. Mori-Nu tofu has been sterilized so all bacteria have been destroyed. Therefore, shelf life is increased, the consumer doesn't have to soak the tofu before using it, and the tofu does not get rancid. Many people who are learning to use tofu unknowingly use rancid tofu. A foolproof way to know that your tofu is fresh is to refrigerate it after purchasing and after opening the box. Once opened, tofu can become rancid, so use within five days. Mori-Nu tofu comes in extra firm, firm, and soft consistencies. The firm Mori-Nu tofu is equivalent to the soft tofu consistency of other brands, because Mori-Nu has a higher moisture content.

FRESH FRUITS:

I purchase a variety of fresh fruits weekly — apples, oranges, seedless red grapes, bananas, and fruits in season. For a treat, our family enjoys a mango or two each week. I love lemon or lime water and also like to use these fruits as a garnish. So I purchase three or four lemons and limes each week.

DRIED FRUITS:

Watch out for fruits that are dried with sulfites. Many people are allergic to sulfites. I use a home food dehydrator, partially drying the fruits and freezing them in airtight bags. This is a real treat.

Apricots

Coconut:

I usually use the sweetened type and limit the quantity; however, the unsweetened type is better if you're trying to limit sugar. It is usually available only in health food stores.

Currants:

These are a nice change from raisins.

Dates (seedless)

Peaches

Pears

Raisins

CANNED FRUITS AND JUICES

Choose fruits that are juice-packed, have no added sugar, and contain no additives.

Cranberry Juice

Lemon Juice

Peaches

Pears

Pineapple Chunks

FROZEN FRUITS AND JUICES

Be sure to buy juices that have no added sugar. When buying frozen fruits, get those that are loose-packed and that can be quickly frozen without added sugar.

Apple Juice Concentrate:

This concentrate is naturally very sweet and can be used to flavor and sweeten many dessert recipes.

Blueberries (whole)

Cranberry Juice Concentrate

Grape Juice Concentrate

Grapefruit Juice Concentrate

Lemon Juice Concentrate

Orange Juice Concentrate

Pineapple Juice Concentrate

Raspberries (whole)

Strawberries (whole or sliced)

REFRIGERATED FRESH VEGETABLES

Most fresh vegetables, of course, should be purchased as close to serving time as possible so that you can eat them at their peak of nutritive value and flavor. Depending on seasonal availability, every week I purchase three or four types of salad greens (usually green leaf lettuce, head lettuce, Bibb lettuce, and spinach), large beefsteak tomatoes, plum tomatoes, carrots, cabbage, cucumbers, avocados, mushrooms, scallions, fresh herbs, and other salad ingredients. I use lots of broccoli, cauliflower, cabbage, zucchini, summer squash, and eggplant for a variety of vegetarian dishes. Fresh steamed vegetables are rarely turned down.

VEGETABLE BIN VEGETABLES

There are a few fresh vegetables that keep well and can be bought ahead. These will last up to a month if refrigerated.

Garlic Cloves:

I go through three or four bulbs per week. You will find that garlic is a great replacement for salt.

Green Chili Peppers

Jalapeño Peppers

Onions:

Sweet white onions are often more acceptable to those who are not exactly crazy about onions.

Potatoes:

I like russet potatoes for baking and the thin-skinned white or red potatoes for boiling or steaming. Russet potatoes work best for baked potato wedges, because the lower sugar content helps to prevent the potato from burning on the outside before the inside is cooked. I also keep a supply of white cooking potatoes on hand for use in recipes in which potatoes will be combined with other foods.

FROZEN VEGETABLES

I keep a supply of frozen vegetables in the freezer just in case I run out of a fresh vegetable.

Broccoli

Carrots (sliced and baby whole)

Cauliflower

Corn

Green Beans

Peas

Spinach (chopped)

CANNED VEGETABLES

Because of the hidden salt usually found in them, I use very few canned vegetables. Tomato paste is the exception. I use my own canned Roma tomatoes for making delicious Italian sauce.

Green Chilies (chopped)

Olives (black)

Pimientos (chopped)

Roasted Red Peppers:

If you are too busy to roast your own, these canned whole roasted red peppers are great to fall back on.

Tomato Paste (low-salt)

Tomatoes (canned diced or chopped, low-salt)

Tomatoes (canned whole with low salt)

TEXTURED VEGETABLE PROTEIN PRODUCTS

Worthington Foods, Loma Linda Foods, Morningstar Farms, and Natural Touch are all name brands of canned and frozen meat substitutes. These products, called "textured vegetable proteins," are made from gluten (protein from wheat flour) and soy products. They are free of animal fat, cholesterol, and preservatives. They are typically lower in fat (especially saturated fat) and calories than their meat and egg counterparts. These foods add a meatlike flavor and texture to recipes. They are nationally available in natural food stores and grocery stores.

DAIRY PRODUCTS AND SUBSTITUTES

Read labels carefully. Buy low-fat milk, cheeses, and sour creams. Skim milk and part-skim cheeses have the lowest fat content. Remember that even 2 percent milk is really 32 percent fat, and that 1 percent milk is really 16 percent fat. Only skim milk is fat-free. The nutrition analysis in this book is based on using skim milk and part-skim cheeses in the low-fat dairy options.

Powdered Tofu Milk:

I like this as a replacement for dairy milk. And it has a smoother texture and better flavor than soy milk. The brands I like are Tofu White, by Magic Mill, and

Smart Shopping

Better Than Milk. Both are available at health food stores. Use this milk to replace dairy milk in recipes, over cereal, and for drinking.

Cheese:
You'll find recipes for nondairy cheese, Parmesan cheese, and whipped cream in the Variations section of this book. Tofu cheese, almond cheese, etc., are available in health food stores, and make good cheese replacements.

Eggs:
Lacto-ovovegetarians and others who need to lower fat and cholesterol in their diet discard the yolks to eliminate cholesterol. One-third cup of tofu blended with a small amount of water until whipped-egg consistency can replace one egg, or 3 tablespoons water mixed with 1 tablespoon cornstarch can replace one egg.

Evaporated Skim Milk:
Although it comes in a can, don't confuse this with canned sweetened condensed milk, a totally different and much less healthy product. Canned evaporated skim milk is a good replacement for cream or half-and-half in recipes. You can even use it to make an acceptable substitute for whipped cream by refrigerating it until it is very cold. Then, adding a little sweetener and vanilla, whip it at high speed with an electric mixer for about six minutes. You'll never miss the extra fat.

Mozzarella Cheese, part-skim:
This is a low-fat cheese that is made without rennin (rennin is from the lining of a calf's stomach and is used in most cheeses). More cheeses are now being made without rennin. Mozzarella cheese can be grated and frozen for future use.

Parmesan Cheese:
Although this cheese is high in fat, a tiny bit adds a lot of flavor and can be substituted for a much larger portion of other cheeses in recipes. In the Variations section of this book there is a substitute for Parmesan cheese.

SEASONINGS AND HERBS

Fresh or Dried Herbs:
Fresh herbs have so much more flavor in recipes than dried herbs, but I keep the dried herbs on hand for times that I cannot get fresh ones. If you can grow your own fresh herbs, that is the best. Just chop the leaves of the fresh herbs and use in recipes at the proportions of three times the amount of dried herbs. For example, 1 teaspoon of dried basil can be replaced with 3 teaspoons of fresh basil. To preserve more of the flavor, store fresh herbs in the refrigerator in a vase of water, and store dried herbs in the freezer or refrigerator. The following herbs and seasonings are the ones I use the most and always try to have on hand in the fresh and dried form.

Basil
Celery Leaves (crushed)
Celery Seed (ground)
Chili Powder
Cinnamon (ground and stick)
Coconut Extract
Coriander
Cumin

Dillweed
George Washington Broth Mix:
This powdered broth mix comes in beefy brown, golden, and onion flavors and is available at health food stores and some grocery stores. It has a vegetable oil base and contains no animal fat.
Fresh Ginger Root or Ginger
Granulated Garlic or Garlic Powder
Lemon Peel (grated)
McKay's Chicken-Style Seasoning:
An excellent chicken-flavored seasoning for broth and soups, this seasoning has a vegetable oil base and contains no animal fat. It is available at health food stores. You can make your own chicken seasoning mix by using the Chicken-like Seasoning recipe in the Variations section of this book.
Mint
Mizo (soybean paste):
Mizo is available at Oriental or health food stores.
Mustard (dried)
Nutritional Yeast Flakes:
This is edible brewer's yeast *(Saccharomyces cerevisiae)* in flake form. Don't confuse it with the brown powdered brewer's yeast product, which is very bitter. These yeast flakes are yellow and have a cheese-like flavor. I use them for seasoning popcorn and wherever a cheese flavor is wanted.
Onion Powder
Oregano Leaves (chopped):
There are two types of oregano—Italian and Mexican. They are very different in taste. Use Italian with Italian foods and

Mexican with Mexican foods.

Paprika:

I prefer Hungarian paprika because of its nice red color.

Parsley (chopped)

Poppy Seeds

Rosemary

Sage

Savory

Soy Sauce (low-salt)

Thyme

Turmeric:

Used to season and add yellow color to foods.

Vanilla Extract (white and regular):
Use white vanilla when flavoring white or light-colored foods, such as ice cream or whipped toppings. It is available in grocery stores in the cake-decorating section. The flavor is the same as regular vanilla. Be sure to use pure vanilla, not imitation.

MISCELLANEOUS

Active Dry Yeast:

Dry yeast comes in two types—regular and rapid-rise. If you use instant yeast, you allow the bread dough to rise only once in bread tins. Be sure to read the label carefully to determine which yeast you are buying. For the best results, use the yeast by the date listed on the package. Store in the refrigerator or freezer to maintain freshness.

Brown Sugar

Cornstarch:

This is used for thickening sauces, soups, and gravies.

Carob Chips:

Carob is the ground dried fruit of the carob tree, which grows principally in the Mediterranean region. Because products made from carob resemble chocolate, some people consider the fruit a chocolate substitute. Carob does not taste as rich as chocolate, but it has its own unique, pleasant flavor. Not only is it low in fat, low in calories, and contains no caffeine, but it is naturally sweet and contains fiber, calcium, phosphorus, and potassium. Carob is available in several forms: as powder, sweetened or unsweetened carob chips, blocks for baking or cooking, and powdered mixes for hot carob beverages. Carob chips are available at some grocery stores and at all health food stores. I use the sweetened carob chips for most of my recipes.

Club Soda:

This low-calorie carbonated beverage makes a sparkling addition to punches.

Honey

Molasses:

Store molasses at room temperature before opening, then keep it in the refrigerator, where it will keep for up to three months. Molasses is available in both light, dark, or blackstrap. I prefer the milder flavor of light molasses.

Nonstick Vegetable Cooking Spray:

I use a nonstick spray (such as Pam) for oiling baking pans or preparing a skillet for sautéing. It is a good way to save on fat without sacrificing flavor.

Tapioca:

Instant brands are the most convenient.

Smart Shopping

Vegetable Oils:

Keep all oils in the refrigerator. Oil kept on the pantry shelf can turn rancid and lose its fresh flavor.

Canola Oil:

Canola oil is made from rapeseed. Like olive oil, it is high in monounsaturated fat, which studies show is the preferred type of fat to lower cholesterol. It is a mild-tasting vegetable oil that does not break down at high temperatures and can be used in all types of cooking. It is quickly gaining popularity at the supermarket.

Olive Oil (cold-pressed):

High in monounsaturated fat, this oil is a good choice for fighting cholesterol. There are several varieties from light all the way to extra-virgin, which is almost green, the color of the olives, and has the strongest taste. I prefer the taste of light olive oil for most cooking. The extra-virgin is perfect for a hearty tomato sauce.

FOR YOUR INFORMATION

MEASUREMENT EQUIVALENTS

3 teaspoons	=	1 tablespoon (15 ml.)
16 tablespoons	=	1 cup (about 250 ml.)
4 tablespoons	=	$\frac{1}{4}$ cup (about 60 ml.)
1 ounce	=	30 milliliters
$\frac{1}{3}$ cup	=	$5\frac{1}{3}$ tablespoons (about 80 ml.)
2 cups	=	1 pint (about 500 ml.)
4 cups (2 pints)	=	1 quart
4 quarts (liquid)	=	1 gallon

SUBSTITUTIONS:

Many of the recipes you are currently using can be adapted to lower their fat content and improve their nutritional value. Experiment to find the alternatives you like best.

Whole Eggs

For recipes that do not need leavening, replace one whole egg with:

- two egg whites.
- Morningstar Farms Better 'n Eggs or $\frac{1}{4}$-$\frac{1}{3}$ cup blended tofu (both are cholesterol-free alternatives).
- 1 tablespoon cornstarch dissolved in 3 tablespoons of water

Sugar

Replace $1\frac{1}{4}$ cups sugar plus $\frac{1}{4}$ cup liquid with 1 cup honey.

Whole Milk

Replace 1 cup fresh whole milk with 1 cup nondairy milk alternative, such as tofu milk, almond milk, or cashew-rice milk.

Sour Cream

Replace sour cream with Tofu Sour Cream (a cholesterol-free, low-fat alternative; recipe in Variations section).

Whipped Cream

Replace whipped cream with Tofu Whipped Cream (a cholesterol-free, low-fat alternative; recipe in the Variations section).

Mayonnaise

Replace mayonnaise with the Soy Ranch Mayonnaise (a cholesterol-free, low-fat nondairy alternative; recipe in the Variations section).

HOW THE RECIPES ARE ANALYZED:

Calories per serving and a nutrient breakdown are included for every recipe. The dairy and nondairy options for each recipe are calculated separately. The nutrients listed include grams of carbohydrate, protein, fat, and fiber. The fat is broken down into polyunsaturated, monounsaturated, saturated, and total fat. The nutrients listed in milligrams include cholesterol, sodium, potassium, iron, and calcium.

The recipes were developed for people who love good food, but who are interested in lowering their intake of calories, sugar, fat, cholesterol, and sodium to maintain healthful eating patterns. The levels of these restricted nutrients in some recipes may be higher than those prescribed by a physician for specific health problems. The calorie and nutrient breakdown of each recipe is derived from computer analysis, based primarily on information from the U.S. Department of Agriculture. The values are as accurate as possible and reflect the following assumptions:

- All nutrient breakdowns are listed per serving.
- When a range is given for the number of servings (example: serves 6-8), the analysis is calculated on the larger number of servings.
- When a range is given for an ingredient (example: 3 to $3\frac{1}{2}$ cups flour) the analysis is calculated on the lesser amount.
- When ingredients are stated as "optional" or "to taste," they have been deleted from the nutrient information.
- When a recipe gives the option of using oil or water, the analysis is based on using water.
- When the recipe gives the option of baking in a pan coated with nonstick vegetable spray, the analysis will be based on the baking option.
- When the recipe calls for honey or sugar, the analysis will be based on honey.
- When the recipe calls for a choice of honey, sugar, or fruit juice, the analysis will be based on fruit juice.
- If a recipe calls for honey or sugar, the recipe will be analyzed with honey.

Nutritional Analysis

						FATS										DIABETIC EXCHANGE					
RECIPE	Serving	Cal	Pro gm	CHO gm	Chol mg	Total gm	Poly gm	Mono gm	Sat gm	Fiber gm	Folate ug	Vit C mg	Na mg	Iron mg	Ca mg	Bread Ex	Meat Ex	Veg Ex	Milk Ex	Fruit Ex	Fat Ex
BREAKFAST																					
Almond-Oat Scones (dairy)	1 scone	226.3	4.413	24.89	0.208	11.51	3.245	6.586	0.916	0.278	5.317	8.601	157.3	1.148	31.48	1.2	0.0	0.0	0.0	0.0	2.3
Almond-Oat Scones (nondairy)	1 scone	227	4.186	25.11	0	11.59	3.244	6.58	0.901	0.278	4.639	8.539	155.9	1.181	16.79	1.2	0.0	0.0	0.1	0.0	2.3
Apple Pancakes (dairy)	2 cakes	115.6	4.346	22.09	0.571	1.389	0.424	0.621	0.169	1.794	8.456	2.019	229.2	0.862	65.64	0.9	0.1	0.0	0.1	0.3	0.2
Apple Pancakes (nondairy)	2 cakes	118.6	2.959	23.36	0	1.841	0.552	0.648	0.16	1.794	6.313	2.019	207.6	1.013	27.06	0.9	0.1	0.0	0.2	0.3	0.4
Belgian Waffles (dairy)	1 waffle	367.4	10.22	56.66	1.667	13.06	3.864	6.947	1.359	5.268	22.5	10.12	483.2	2.466	124	1.5	0.5	0.0	0.1	1.5	2.2
Belgian Waffles (nondairy)	1 waffle	368.8	9.386	58.05	0	12.96	3.848	6.822	1.091	5.268	20.5	10.13	476	2.566	77.38	1.5	0.5	0.0	0.3	1.5	2.2
Apricot Sauce	1/4 cup	72.55	0.951	18.66	0	0.06	0.01	0.026	0.004	1.963	2.573	7.438	6.048	0.454	18.17	0.0	0.0	0.0	0.0	1.2	0.0
Breakfast Burritos (dairy)	1 burrito	275.4	11.54	49.65	0	3.82	1.584	1.197	0.602	2.526	22.76	24.62	584.3	2.656	131.5	2.9	0.6	0.9	0.1	0.0	0.5
Breakfast Burritos (nondairy)	1 burrito	295.9	14.62	46.28	0	7.57	3.193	2.879	0.977	3.539	15.42	14.09	769.1	3.987	83.83	4.0	1.4	0.0	0.0	0.0	2.8
Cheryl's Almond Granola	1/4 cup	150.4	4.65	25.8	0	3.79	.93	1.87	.41	2.84	7.62	14.26	57.6	1.33	21.05	.85	0.0	0.0	0.0	.48	.75
Choles.-free Pancakes (dairy)	2 cakes	210.2	7.142	30.95	1.667	6.785	2.327	3.12	0.833	2.236	12.51	0.784	462.7	1.667	100.2	1.5	0.3	0.0	0.1	0.0	1.3
Choles.-free Pancakes (nondairy)	2 cakes	209.8	6.47	31.66	0	6.686	2.311	2.995	0.565	2.236	10.51	0.589	458.9	1.767	53.56	1.5	0.3	0.0	0.2	0.0	1.3
Currant-Sesame Scones (dairy)	1 scone	211	4.166	24.01	0.181	11.07	3.187	5.763	0.817	1.683	2.759	8.567	155.9	1.406	45.38	1.2	0.0	0.0	0.0	0.0	2.2
Currant-Sesame Scones (nondairy)	1 scone	212	3.924	24.38	0	11.14	3.186	5.758	0.804	1.683	2.172	8.567	153.8	1.434	32.65	1.2	0.0	0.0	0.1	0.0	2.2
Five-Grain Cooked Cereal	1/2 cup	179.2	6.02	35.56	0	1.74	.639	.4075	.3655	4.35	18.76	.471	180.3	2.003	18.55	2.1	0.0	0.0	0.0	.25	.1
Low-Fat Granola	1/2 cup	341.5	8.491	62.33	0	7.769	4.303	1.792	0.797	4.75	27.75	38.42	14.84	2.777	48.57	1.8	0.1	0.0	0.0	1.7	1.4
Peach-Berry-Banana Fruit Shake (dairy)	1 cup	213.2	8.368	45.35	2	0.836	0.16	0.148	0.275	3.155	97.59	81.48	88.93	0.667	248	0.0	0.0	0.0	0.7	2.1	0.0
Peach-Berry-Banana Fruit Shake (nondairy)	1 cup	281.8	7.521	41.07	0	10.87	3.532	5.678	1.016	3.18	84.25	82.83	437.8	1.376	58.77	0.1	0.8	0.0	0.0	2.2	1.8
Peach or Apricot Butter	2 tbsp	10.4	.10	2.63	0	.02	.005	.005	.002	-	.108	3.73	.907	.141	1.67	0.0	0.0	0.0	0.0	.175	0.0
Pineapple-Banana Breakfast Shake (dairy)	1 cup	189.2	7.747	39.76	1.33	1.134	0.098	0.086	0.203	3.804	33.74	34.07	61.48	1.471	179.4	0.2	0.0	0.0	0.5	2.1	0.1
Pineapple-Banana Breakfast Shake (nondairy)	1 cup	237.8	7.311	37.02	0	8.035	2.417	3.89	0.715	3.821	24.89	35.02	303.3	1.961	54.4	0.3	0.5	0.0	0.0	2.1	1.4
Quick-cooking Seven-Grain Cereal	1 1/4 cups	186.5	7.523	34.93	0.5	2.453	0.828	0.716	0.443	3.89	13.26	0.599	157.8	1.734	61.49	1.7	0.0	0.0	0.1	0.5	0.5
Red Berry Spread	2 tsp	6.009	0.065	1.482	0	0.038	0.02	0.005	0.002	0.255	1.767	4.485	0.119	0.044	1.812	0.0	0.0	0.0	0.0	0.0	0.0
LUNCH: SANDWICHES																					
Garbanzo Bean Sandwiches	1 pita	341.1	13.67	58.7	0.031	7.913	3.46	2.657	0.97	10.67	40.52	19.99	874.8	5.324	87.1	4.0	0.1	0.5	0.0	0.0	1.2
Grilled Vegetable Sandwich With Creamy Herb Dressing	1 sandwich	398.8	8.813	46.91	0	20.9	0.96	5.599	3.251	4.278	54.95	303.3	586.4	44.83	94.57	1.8	0.3	3.4	0.0	0.1	4.5
Guilt-free Burgers	3" burger	156.9	6.114	27.85	0	3.067	1.284	0.503	0.232	2.83	7.899	1.442	69.62	0.98	16.29	1.8	0.1	0.1	0.0	0.0	0.6

Item	Serving																					
Ital.-Style Vegetarian Hoagie	4"sandwich	222.4	5.971	28.48	0	9.59	1.999	13.5	2.702	2.546	95	27.45	417.8	2.348	82.13	1.6	0.0	0.0	1.0	0.0	0.0	3.8
Lentil Patties	1 pita half	171.3	11.87	30.8	0	.58	.227	.195	.096	1.07	33.8	5.53	101.9	3.28	29.99	1.87	.96	0.0	.32	0.0	0.0	0.0
Mexican Chili Burgers	1 burger	100.7	3.712	19.19	0	1.269	.507	.238	.164	1.842	7.576	3.585	63.92	0.86	31.34	1.0	0.2	0.0	0.6	0.0	0.0	0.4
Oven-baked Mexi-Fries	1/2 cup	289.8	5.59	59.81	0	3.95	1.135	2.007	.319	7.071	24.85	35.84	27.52	1.235	21.95	3.7	0.0	0.0	0.0	0.0	0.0	0.7
Oven-baked Seasoned Fries	1/2 cup	285	5.414	59.06	0	3.682	1.125	2.005	.314	4.095	24.85	35	13.74	0.965	13.9	3.7	0.0	0.0	0.0	0.0	0.0	0.7
Roasted Vegetable Pitas With Creamy Herb Dressing	2 pita halves	273.6	10.47	55.4	0	5.751	0.56	2.56	0.575	10.39	138.9	1184	89.28	171.9	129	0.2	0.0	0.0	9.8	0.0	0.0	1.1
Toasted Bagels With Roasted Red Pepper Spread	2 bagel halves	310.1	13.78	58.73	0.063	3.598	1.505	0.456	0.386	3.194	55.83	446.8	485.4	67.32	106.7	2.6	0.3	0.0	3.4	0.0	0.0	0.7

LUNCH: SENSATIONAL MAIN DISH SALADS

Item	Serving																					
Haystacks	1 cup	180	3.58	33.87	0	2.4	.02	.01	.012	2.23	19.49	3.04	262.7	.3	14.7	1.05	.025	.03	.117	1.2	.47	
Summer Harvest Chicken-Potato Salad	1/2 cup	261.1	9.925	48.17	0.333	3.815	2.221	.86	.514	3.987	38.06	117	381.3	15.76	100.4	2.8	0.6	0.1	0.9	0.0	0.0	0.4
Soy Ranch Dressing	1 tbsp	39.55	0.097	1.539	0	3.831	1.189	2.09	.292	.0121	0.448	.27	18.25	0.048	2.303	0.0	0.0	0.0	0.0	0.0	0.0	0.8
Waldorf Potato Salad	1/2 cup	227.6	2.50	35.15	0	9.4	2.78	5.34	.705	3.379	13.5	9.21	45.55	.572	16.91	1.45	0.0	0.5	.05	.55	1.85	

LUNCH: SOUPS

Item	Serving																					
Chilled Chunky Gazpacho	1 cup	94.06	3.575	18.19	0	2.345	0.391	1.332	0.323	3.654	42.82	30.88	453	2.123	78.76	0.1	0.0	0.0	3.0	0.0	0.0	0.3
Chilled Minted Pea Soup	1 1/2 cups	216.6	10.67	25.91	0	8.391	1.69	5.265	0.962	9.369	124.2	12.53	183.7	2.313	53.17	1.4	0.9	0.0	0.5	0.0	0.0	1.5
Creamy Broccoli-Rice Soup	1 1/2 cups	140.1	6.652	27.3	1	1.091	0.373	0.294	0.251	4.323	95.24	75.02	80.46	1.348	129.4	1.2	0.0	0.2	1.0	0.0	0.0	0.0
Creamy Garlic Potato Soup	1 cup	175.6	3.907	33.42	0	2.401	0.25	1.666	0.339	2.937	13.42	16.3	69.98	0.58	69.47	1.6	0.0	0.5	0.3	0.0	0.0	0.5
Italian Vegetable Soup	1 cup	98.9	5.1	19.6	0	.5	.119	.033	.046	4.02	23.31	12.72	140.1	1.83	43.76	.95	0.0	0.0	.95	0.0	0.0	0.0
Vegetable Chili	1 cup	250.1	11.8	49	0	2.004	5.67	.354	.228	12.26	115.75	28.35	562.5	45.9	37.75	2.1	.3	0.0	.36	0.0	0.0	.1
Vegetable Split-Pea Soup	1 1/2 cups	181.2	12.49	32.76	0	0.632	0.267	0.126	0.09	13.2	141.2	3.35	41.67	2.356	41.19	2.0	0.9	0.0	0.5	0.0	0.0	0.0

MAIN DISH DINNERS: PASTA

Item	Serving																					
Angel Hair Vegetable Toss	1 1/2 cups	391.2	17.54	74.52	95.68	3.921	0.338	0.039	1.186	11.48	143	105.3	333.3	6.873	175.6	3.3	0.0	0.0	4.5	0.0	0.0	0.6
Asparagus "Alfredo" Pasta Bows	1 cup	162	6.361	16.71	0.167	8.866	1.453	5.252	1.153	2.846	54.73	72.31	209.5	1.398	64.18	0.5	0.4	0.0	0.8	0.0	0.0	2.2
Chili Macaroni	1 cup	162.7	10.63	22.9	4.51	4.168	2.3	.952	.621	5.96	38.4	53	53.25	2.548	57.05	.9	.85	0.0	1.45	0.0	0.0	.25
Fresh Basil Pesto With Pasta	1 cup	544.7	16.05	67.17	0	25.38	6.113	14.07	3.629	3.004	27.22	0.861	7.26	5.262	31.59	4.1	0.0	0.1	0.0	0.0	0.0	5.0
Linguine With Fresh Tomato Sauce	1 cup	467.6	19.69	97.38	63.37	5.024	0.04	0.008	0.675	12.67	131.2	15.62	513.3	230	206.7	2.1	0.0	0.0	13.1	0.0	0.0	1.1
Pasta Tossed With Seasoned Olive Oil and Fresh Basil	1 cup	221	8.688	41.03	63.37	2.801	0.072	0.017	0.68	3.095	14.16	16.14	278.9	3.251	93.72	2.1	0.0	0.0	1.7	0.0	0.0	0.05
Pasta With Basil and Tomatoes	1 cup	168.4	4.614	22.72	0	5.806	0.637	4.029	0.78	2.135	4.543	9.826	353.7	1.424	55.85	1.0	1.3	0.0	0.0	0.0	0.0	1.1
Sun-dried Tomato-Red Pepper Pesto With Pasta	1 cup	299	13.2	61.8	0	5.88	.71	2.73	.889	7.02	131.5	427.8	138.65	103.5	381	.525	.875	9.125	0.0	0.0	0.0	.95

FATS   **DIABETIC EXCHANGE**

RECIPE	Serving	Cal	Pro gm	CHO gm	Chol mg	Total gm	Poly gm	Mono gm	Sat gm	Fiber gm	Folate ug	Vit C mg	Na mg	Iron mg	Ca Ex	Bread Ex	Meat Ex	Veg Ex	Milk Ex	Fruit Ex	Fat Ex
Vegetable Lasagna	2½" sq.	275.4	8.114	50.2	0.346	4.231	0.836	2.193	0.521	5.385	42.77	265.9	334.3	36.87	97.42	1.7	0.2	3.7	0.0	0.0	0.8
Vermicelli With Chunky Vegetable Sauce	1½ cups	434.6	17.22	92.2	0	2.459	0.549	0.159	0.2	10.69	96.92	803.6	695	117.7	151.2	2.8	0.0	8.2	0.0	0.0	0.3

MAIN DISH DINNERS: RICE AND COUSCOUS

RECIPE	Serving	Cal	Pro gm	CHO gm	Chol mg	Total gm	Poly gm	Mono gm	Sat gm	Fiber gm	Folate ug	Vit C mg	Na mg	Iron mg	Ca Ex	Bread Ex	Meat Ex	Veg Ex	Milk Ex	Fruit Ex	Fat Ex
Basil-roasted Vegetables Over Couscous	2 cups	255.6	7.554	52.12	0	4.229	0.39	2.507	0.497	7.934	28.39	77.96	148.7	1	33.94	2.2	0.0	1.7	0.0	0.0	0.7
Basmati Rice Seasoned With Dried Fruits and Nuts	1 cup	321.3	4.47	50.99	0	12.21	1.917	7.136	1.114	3.332	7.454	2.165	268.9	0.924	17.55	2.4	0.0	0.2	0.0	0.8	2.4
Brown Rice With Vegetables and Tomato Pesto	1 cup	150.1	4.166	30.95	0	1.825	0.508	0.784	0.309	3.637	35.28	33.33	81.33	1.252	45.86	1.4	0.0	1.6	0.0	0.0	0.2
Couscous Alfresco	1½ cups	453.4	14.62	93.57	0	5.384	1.929	2.458	0.604	13.34	176.2	24.55	147.3	1.442	39.32	4.5	0.1	1.6	0.0	0.0	1.0
Curried "Chicken" and Broccoli Couscous	1½ cups	394.8	16.83	70.36	0	8.411	3.381	2.921	0.952	11.05	93.76	618.9	342.5	86.86	77.42	2.3	0.9	4.7	0.0	0.0	1.2
Garden Vegetable Couscous	1 cup	208	7.89	36.035	0	4.112	1.50	1.81	.545	6.48	38.65	12.25	261.95	2.33	60.75	2.05	.15	1.25	0.0	0.0	.5
Grilled Vegetables Over Rice	1 cup	230.5	8.23	42.88	0	3.447	1.13	1.298	.479	7.505	154.4	23.86	19.125	2.36	54.65	2.5	0.0	.8	0.0	0.0	.4
Hearty Rice Skillet	1 cup	224.7	9.67	41.25	0	3.41	.887	1.8	.437	7.83	103.4	15.35	153.9	2.529	49.48	2.25	.35	.8	0.0	0.0	.5
Herbed "Chicken" Couscous and Vegetables	1 cup	238	12.71	31.88	0	6.592	3.647	1.972	0.781	4.242	37.42	11.49	309	1.939	33.25	2.0	0.9	0.3	0.0	0.0	0.7
Pesto Rice and Beans	1 cup	524	21.8	56.32	0	25.88	12.88	9.259	2.373	3.043	230.1	6.365	80.65	5.217	127.9	3.3	1.7	0.4	0.0	0.0	4.9
Pesto Risotto	1 cup	135.62	4.527	19.87	0	5.10	2.278	10.27	1.942	1.847	54.51	14.61	25.3	1.132	24.45	1.2	0.0	0.2	0.0	0.0	3.0
Roasted-Pepper Bruschetta	1 piece	107.2	3.478	18.12	0	2.507	0.532	1.239	0.439	2.338	9.237	65.48	176.3	1.2	32.24	1.0	0.0	0.6	0.0	0.0	0.5
Spring Vegetable Curry	1 cup	435	14.05	64.61	0	15.03	0.987	2.271	10.1	11.47	131.4	33.69	128.1	3.627	86.34	3.3	0.5	1.6	0.0	0.0	2.4
Stir-fried Asian Vegetables	1 cup	315.3	8.216	61.12	0	5.752	2.251	2.232	0.655	2.042	35.32	20.12	265.9	2.565	35.63	3.6	0.0	1.2	0.0	0.0	1.1
Teriyaki Stir-Fry Over Rice	1½ cups	385	11.05	80.98	0	6.035	2.637	6.619	1.641	7.204	74.04	398.6	1812	59.1	83.99	2.5	0.3	3.6	0.0	0.0	2.1
Vegetable Medley Quiche in Rice Crust	1 piece	219.2	9.746	34.94	0	5.367	1.699	2.376	0.809	4.309	46.66	67.85	229.8	2.116	75.32	2.7	1.2	1.0	0.0	0.0	1.9

MAIN DISH DINNERS: POTATOES

RECIPE	Serving	Cal	Pro gm	CHO gm	Chol mg	Total gm	Poly gm	Mono gm	Sat gm	Fiber gm	Folate ug	Vit C mg	Na mg	Iron mg	Ca Ex	Bread Ex	Meat Ex	Veg Ex	Milk Ex	Fruit Ex	Fat Ex
Cheesy Potato Skins (dairy)	½ cup	145.5	5.41	18.21	7.98	5.95	.498	3.166	1.93	1.898	9.41	10.9	104	.433	100.1	1.05	.5	0.0	0.0	0.0	.8
Garden-fresh Potato Toss	1 cup	250	6.002	56.08		1.125	0.206	0.569	0.183	6.29	40.4	55.19	19.46	3.339	41.24	2.9	0.0	0.9	0.0	0.0	0.2
Garlic Potatoes With "Chicken"	1 cup	226.2	7.716	36.84	5.857	5.857	2.36	2.501	0.77	4.62	18.92	22.83	200.1	1.213	32.32	2.1	0.6	0.6	0.0	0.0	0.8
Mexican Baked Potatoes With Bean-and-Corn Salsa	1 potato	385.5	22.5	70.72	7.986	3.466	0.478	0.753	1.503	12.11	127.4	322.2	702.5	45.73	304.1	3.8	1.7	2.3	0.0	0.0	0.2
Roots at 500°F	1 cup	195.84	2.648	42.05	0	2.32	0.657	4.986	0.957	1.72	31.75	19.13	40.52	0.847	25.24	2.1	0.0	0.5	0.0	0.0	1.4
Vegetable Potato Salad	1 cup	145.3	5.943	29.31	0.25	0.88	0.179	0.021	0.108	4.706	153.1	45.72	235.1	1.249	60.37	1.3	0.0	1.2	0.1	0.0	0.0

MAIN DISH DINNERS: MEXICAN

Item	Serving																			
Baked Enchilada Casserole	3" square	290.7	16.42	40.39	19.96	6.72	0.548	3.18	5.873	71.97	7.17	329.2	3.296	309.6	2.4	1.5	0.5	0.0	0.0	0.3
Bean Enchiladas	1 enchilada	290.4	16.04	41.66	0	6.261	1.855	0.908	2.724	57.69	36.32	858	3.543	220.3	2.6	1.2	1.3	0.0	0.0	1.7
Layered Bean Dip	1/2 cup	194.5	9.346	29.77	0	5.24	1.193	0.928	7.452	135.4	135.5	730.5	22.13	112.7	1.8	0.6	0.1	0.0	0.0	1.1
No-Guilt Refried Beans	1/2 cup	100.1	5.701	19	0	0.42	0.15	0.084	4.458	74.34	3.334	533.8	2.024	48.67	1.1	0.2	0.2	0.0	0.0	0.0
Oven-baked Vegetable Fajitas	1 fajita	375.3	14.76	70.97	0.25	6.358	1.475	1.359	13.14	32.91	8.028	829.1	3.453	134.3	4.2	0.0	1.6	0.0	0.0	0.7
Tamale Pie	1 cup	428.9	8.409	83.75	0	7.321	1.676	2.018	6.033	50.59	13.02	1465	3.007	67.37	4.1	0.0	2.2	0.0	0.3	1.3
Vegetable Burritos Grande	1 burrito	294.4	13.75	46.45	7.986	7.025	1.39	2.149	7.302	114.1	27.36	500.6	2.976	174.4	2.7	0.8	1.0	0.0	0.0	0.9
White Bean Quesadillas	1 quesadilla	293.9	19.09	51.56	19.96	3.77	4.103	3.579	4.523	113.6	681	302.7	87.96	117.2	2.1	1.2	4.1	0.0	0.0	1.5

MAIN DISH DINNERS: LEGUMES

Item	Serving																			
Indian Lentils and Rice	1 1/2 cups	373.9	19.67	57.93	0	7.781	2.253	1.684	2.945	259.7	22.06	431.4	6.882	92.05	3.5	1.6	0.4	0.0	0.0	1.1
Mazidra	1/2 cup	121.5	7.13	16.12	0	3.65	0.406	0.494	0.429	112.3	4.686	277	2.29	24.86	0.9	0.6	0.4	0.0	0.0	0.7

MAIN DISH DINNERS: PIZZA

Item	Serving																			
French Bread Pizza With Beans and Chunky Vegetables	5" piece	324.3	13.38	57.79	0	5.4	2.051	2.192	6.218	130.8	157.1	939	32.79	139.9	3.4	0.6	0.9	0.0	0.0	2.2
Fresh Tomato-Herb Pizza	1 piece	425	21.17	69.77	0	12.05	6.285	5.064	14.3	309.8	757.1	916.9	120.1	283.3	3.0	1.9	1.5	0.0	0.1	6.6
Grilled Vegetable Pizza With Spinach-Walnut Pesto	1 piece	145.2	3.978	24	0	3.884	0.663	0.526	2.034	70.01	8.38	42.05	1.882	36.83	1.3	0.0	0.4	0.0	0.0	0.7
Pesto Pizza	1 piece	175.4	4.698	26.4	0	6.414	1.341	0.892	2.115	28.23	2.52	104.1	1.931	43.7	1.3	0.0	0.7	0.0	0.0	1.2
Roasted Vegetable Pizza	1 piece	350	15.95	54.97	0	12.42	5.332	4.339	10.45	266.7	653.6	447.5	100.2	189.7	2.9	1.6	0.5	0.0	0.1	5.6
Spinach-Pesto Salad Pizza	1 piece	316.9	11.61	21.38	0	11.75	5.416	3.271	2.949	81.28	47.09	73.96	4.061	78.91	0.7	0.7	1.1	0.0	0.1	4.3

DESSERTS

Item	Serving																			
Blueberry Crisp	1 piece	330.25	4.475	56.96	0	10.87	3.48	1.02	2.974	14.99	12.63	17.53	1.726	28.49	1.1	0.1	0.0	0.0	1.9	2.3
Fresh Apple-Pineapple Cream Pie (dairy)	1 piece	247.7	5.646	36.2	1.023	9.595	2.832	0.78	2.266	15.26	3.42	111.4	1.128	128.9	1.0	0.0	0.0	0.3	1.1	1.8
Fresh Apple-Pineapple Cream Pie (nondairy)	1 piece	227.12	5.258	37.6	0	7.02	4.465	1.128	2.287	8.584	3.88	215.7	1.531	29.19	1.6	0.7	0.0	0.0	1.1	3.3
Glazed Fresh Peach Pie	1 piece	245.6	2.91	39.38	0	9.303	2.796	0.683	3.164	9.41	8.4	68.8	0.976	11.05	1.1	0.0	0.0	0.0	0.9	1.8
Glazed Fresh Strawberry Pie	1 piece	224.3	2.699	33.08	0	9.602	2.946	0.693	2.624	24.88	63.38	69.91	1.26	20.34	1.1	0.0	0.0	0.0	0.5	1.8
Low-Fat Raspberry Cheesecake	1 piece	167.3	2.393	29.34	0.333	4.746	1.425	0.365	1.08	8.094	3.053	49.09	0.721	56.31	0.6	0.0	0.0	0.1	0.1	0.9
Peanut Butter Cookies	1 cookie	62.54	1.297	8.058	0	3.076	0.895	0.481	0.416	4.288	0.245	31.85	0.257	5.31	0.4	0.0	0.0	0.0	0.1	0.5
Pumpkin Pie	1 piece	294.2	3.558	47.57	0	10.49	2.781	1.723	2.31	13.42	2.348	210.5	1.989	32.45	3.0	0.0	0.0	0.0	0.0	2.0
Strawberry-Almond Torte	1 piece	341.4	9.281	52.03	0	11.04	6.1	1.763	2.029	19.8	26.36	217.8	1.974	55.01	1.1	0.8	0.0	0.0	0.5	3.6

FATS / DIABETIC EXCHANGE

RECIPE	Serving	Cal	Pro gm	CHO gm	Chol mg	Total gm	Poly gm	Mono gm	Sat gm	Fiber gm	Folate ug	Vit C mg	Na mg	Iron mg	Ca	Bread Ex	Meat Ex	Veg Ex	Milk Ex	Fruit Ex	Fat Ex
VARIATIONS AND SUBSTITUTIONS																					
Basil-Pine Nut Pesto	2 tbsp	94.91	1.678	1.316	0	10.11	1.979	5.219	1.426	0.07	1.227	0.84	0.206	0.701	6.087	0.0	0.0	0.0	0.0	0.0	0.0
Cheeseless "Cheese" Sauce	3 tbsp	88.84	3.179	9.283	0	5.316	1.16	2.767	0.939	1.963	56.68	147	78.92	22.38	36.82	0.5	0.3	0.0	0.0	0.0	1.2
Cheeseless "Parmesan" Cheese	1 tbsp	40.52	2.383	3.083	0	2.238	0.981	0.844	0.313	1.807	161	0.457	15.25	1.37	53.17	0.0	0.0	0.0	0.0	0.0	0.4
Chicken-like Seasoning	1/4 tsp	0	0	0	0	0	0	0	0	0	0	0	0	0	0	0.1	0.0	0.1	0.0	0.0	0.0
Classic Fresh Salsa	1/4 cup	39.35	1.745	8.665	0	0.448	0.181	0.068	0.064	2.033	7.498	31.96	348	1.133	69.59	0.0	0.0	1.7	0.0	0.0	0.0
Creamy Cucumber Dressing	1 tbsp	14.8	0.315	0.657	0.021	1.269	0.171	0.851	0.173	0.002	0.937	0.556	23.34	0.062	4.045	0.0	0.0	0.0	0.0	0.0	0.3
Creamy Herb Dressing	1 tbsp	21.33	0.414	0.836	0.031	1.891	0.252	1.277	0.256	0.007	0.382	0.913	34.84	0.07	4.812	0.0	0.1	0.0	0.0	0.0	0.5
Nondairy Creamy Onion-Dill Dressing	1 tbsp	21.63	0.394	0.865	0	1.917	0.256	1.28	0.251	0.025	0.562	0.456	34.6	0.102	3.805	0.0	0.0	0.0	0.0	0.0	0.4
Ranch Soy Mayonnaise	1 tsp	7.469	0.023	0.403	0	0.665	0.198	0.348	0.049	0.003	0.1	0.296	2.756	0.005	0.205	0.0	0.0	0.0	0.0	0.0	0.1
Spinach-Walnut Pesto (dairy)	2 tbsp	23.49	0.911	0.898	0.063	1.983	0.816	0.873	0.193	0.265	15.45	2.269	8.353	0.273	16.31	0.0	0.0	0.1	0.0	0.0	0.4
Spinach-Walnut Pesto (nondairy)	2 tbsp	25.6	.884	.764	0	2.29	.921	1.046	.216	.266	14.8	2.25	19.24	.285	10.4	0.0	.025	.075	0.0	0.0	.45
Sweet-and-Sour Sauce	2 tbsp	24.56	0.124	6.162	0	0.038	0.012	0.003	0.005	0.04	4.731	12.92	5.803	0.111	4.638	0.0	0.0	0.0	0.0	0.4	0.0
Tartar Sauce	1 tbsp	13.45	0.299	1.289	0	0.853	0.297	0.434	0.069	0.042	0.577	0.828	40.44	0.057	2.507	0.0	0.0	0.0	0.0	0.0	0.2
Thick and Chunky Salsa	1/4 cup	64.05	2.498	15.06	0	0.403	0.153	0.055	0.057	2.654	21.27	33.25	529	1.188	48.19	0.0	0.0	2.4	0.0	0.0	0.0
Tofu Whipped Cream	2 tbsp	42.64	1.407	3.316	0	2.552	0.841	1.39	0.218	0.011	0.027	0.097	41.18	0.214	8.759	0.0	0.2	0.0	0.0	0.1	0.5
Tofu Yogurt or Sour Cream	1 tbsp	39.53	1.693	1.319	0	3.063	1.009	1.668	0.261	0.008	0.197	0.7	130.3	0.242	10.98	0.0	0.2	0.0	0.0	0.0	0.5
Vinegar-free Tomato Ketchup	1 tbsp	13.6	0.527	3.018	0	0.061	0.021	0.012	0.008	0.622	3.755	7.72	71.58	0.191	9.132	0.0	0.0	0.4	0.0	0.0	0.0

Index of Recipes

"Alfredo" Sauce	69
Almond Torte Crust	119
Almond Torte Filling	119
Almond-Oat Scones	33
Angel Hair Vegetable Toss	68
Apple Pancakes	30
Apricot Sauce	29
Asparagus "Alfredo" Pasta Bows	67
Baked Enchilada Casserole	96
Basil-Pine Nut Pesto	124
Basil-roasted Vegetables Over Couscous	83
Basmati Rice Seasoned With Dried Fruits and Nuts	85
Bean Enchiladas	95
Bean-and-Corn Salsa	93
Belgian Waffles	29
Blueberry Crisp	112
Breakfast Burritos	27
Breakfast Scones With Fruit Butter and Fruit Platter	33, 34
Breakfast Shakes	32, 33
Brown Rice With Vegetables and Tomato Pesto	73
Caesar Salad	52
Caesar Salad Dressing	53
Cheeseless "Cheese" Sauce	127
Cheeseless "Parmesan" Cheese	127
Cheesy Potato Skins	91
Cheryl's Almond Granola	32
Chicken-like Seasoning	121
Chili Macaroni	63
Chili Powder Substitute	121
Chilled Chunky Gazpacho	58
Chilled Minted Pea Soup	57
Cholesterol-free Pancakes	30
Cinnamon Substitute	121
Classic Fresh Salsa	125
Couscous Alfresco	80
Creamy Broccoli-Rice Soup	58
Creamy Cucumber Dressing	124
Creamy Garlic Potato Soup	59
Creamy Herb Dressing	124
Crumb Topping	112
Currant-Sesame Scones	34
Curried "Chicken" and Broccoli Couscous	81
Curry Powder	75
Fettuccine Primavera "Alfredo"	69
Five-Grain Cooked Cereal	35
French Bread Pizza With Beans and Chunky Vegetables	109
Fresh Apple-Pineapple Cream Pie	113
Fresh Basil Pesto With Pasta	67
Fresh Fruit Sauce	37
Fresh Tomato-Herb Pizza	106
Freshly Made Croutons	52
Fruit Salad	37
Garbanzo Bean Sandwiches	45
Garden Greek Salad	55
Garden Vegetable Couscous	80
Garden-fresh Potato Toss	89
Garlic Potatoes With "Chicken"	90
Glazed Fresh Peach Pie	115
Glazed Fresh Strawberry Pie	111
Greek Salad Dressing	55
Grilled Vegetable Pizza With Spinach-Walnut Pesto	105
Grilled Vegetable Sandwich With Creamy Herb Dressing	39
Grilled Vegetables Over Rice	78
Guacamole	126
Guilt-free Burgers	44
Haystacks	53
Hearty Rice Skillet	79
Herbed "Chicken" Couscous and Vegetables	79
Herbed Pizza Crust	107
Herbed Tofu Cheese	71
Indian Lentils and Rice	101
Italian Spice Blend	52
Italian-Style Vegetarian Hoagie	43
Italian Vegetable Soup	61
Layered Bean Dip	97

Lentil Patties	42
Lentil Patties in Pita Pockets With Creamy Cucumber Dressing	42
Linguine With Fresh Tomato Sauce	65
Low-Fat Creamy Onion-Dill Dressing	122
Low-Fat Granola	31
Low-Fat Raspberry Cheesecake	117
Marinade	39
Mazidra	101
Mexican Baked Potatoes With Bean-and-Corn Salsa	93
Mexican Chili Burgers	47
Muesli-Nut Fruit Salad	37
Muesli-Nut Topping	37
No-Guilt Refried Beans	100
Nondairy Creamy Onion-Dill Dressing	123
Oven-baked Mexi-Fries	47
Oven-baked Seasoned Fries	43
Oven-baked Vegetable Fajitas	99
Pasta Tossed With Seasoned Olive Oil and Fresh Basil	68
Pasta With Basil and Tomatoes	63
Pastry Crust	115
Peach or Apricot Butter	35
Peach-Berry-Banana Fruit Shake	33
Peanut Butter Cookies	111
Pesto Pizza	106
Pesto Rice and Beans	74
Pesto Risotto	84
Pesto Sauce	84, 106
Pineapple-Banana Breakfast Shake	32
Pumpkin Pie	112
Quick Pizza Dough	103
Quick-cooking Seven-Grain Cereal	35
Ranch Soy Mayonnaise	123
Red Berry Spread	34
Roasted Vegetable Pitas With Creamy Herb Dressing	41
Roasted Vegetable Pizza	103
Roasted-Pepper Bruschetta	83
Roots at 500°F	89
Soy Ranch Dressing	51
Spinach-Pesto Salad Pizza	105
Spinach-Walnut Pesto	125
Spring Vegetable Curry	75
Stir-fried Asian Vegetables	74
Stir-fry Tips	77
Strawberry-Almond Torte	119
Summer Harvest Chicken-Potato Salad	51
Sun-dried Tomato-Red Pepper Pesto With Pasta	64
Sweet-and-Sour Sauce	126
Tamale Pie	100
Tartar Sauce	126
Teriyaki Sauce	77
Teriyaki Stir-Fry Over Rice	77
Thick and Chunky Salsa	125
Toasted Bagels With Roasted Red Pepper Spread	45
Tofu Cheese	95
Tofu Filling	87
Tofu Whipped Cream	122
Tofu Whipped Topping	119
Tofu Yogurt	117
Tofu Yogurt or Sour Cream	122
Tomato Pesto	73
Vegetable Burritos Grande	96
Vegetable Chili	59
Vegetable Lasagna	71
Vegetable Medley Quiche in Rice Crust	87
Vegetable Potato Salad	90
Vegetable Split-Pea Soup	57
Vegetable Tomato Sauce	71
Vermicelli With Chunky Vegetable Sauce	64
Vinegar-free Tomato Ketchup	127
Waldorf Potato Salad	49
Waldorf Potato Salad Dressing	49
Whipped Topping	119
White Bean Quesadillas	97
Yogurt Cheese	53
Yogurt Ranch Dressing	51

Cheryl D. Thomas Peters, Dietitian
James A. Peters, M.D., Dr. P.H., R.D., R.R.T., F.A.C.P.M.
Nutrition & Lifestyle Medical Clinic
1007 Calimesa Blvd., Suite F.
Calimesa, CA 92320
(909) 795-7300
www.nutrition&lifestyle.com

Contact us to subscribe to our monthly Nutrition & Lifestyle Newsletter, which will include the most recent nutrition updates, new recipes, cooking tips, and other health and exercise information. We specialize in preventive medicine, and are available for Nutrition and Lifestyle seminars, lectures, and cooking classes conducted at our clinic or your location. Visit us on our web page for the latest information, or call our clinic number.